PUSH

Praise – Pray – Persist Until Something Happens

PUSH

Praise – Pray – Persist Until Something Happens

JERRY BONSU

Copyright © 2013 Jerry Bonsu

All rights reserved. No part of this publication may be reproduced without the written permission of the publisher, with the exception of brief excerpts in magazines, articles, reviews, etc.

PUSH

Published in France by VICTORY LIFE MEDIA an imprint of JBM

JERRY BONSU MINISTRIES

http://www.jerrybonsu.org
E-mail: info@jerrybonsu.org

French National Library-in-Publication Data
Dépôt légal: 1/2013

Cover Design by Lisa Hainline
Cover Photo by Bryan Stupar

Printed in the USA

ISBN: 978-2-9541960-1-5

Unless otherwise noted, Scripture quotations are from the King James Version of the Bible.

For further information or permission, contact us on the Internet:

VICTORY LIFE MEDIA *"Empowering our Generation for the next Generation"* www.victorylifemedia.com

Dedication

To my precious daughters Janelle Kierra and Janessa Kimani and to my lovely wife Laetitia.

To my family, mentors, and friends.

Also to the Jerry Bonsu Ministries Team and the VLIC (Victory Life International Center) family.

CONTENTS

INTRODUCTION 9

PART I

Praise Until Something Happens

CHAPTER 1	WHAT IS PRAISE?	15
CHAPTER 2	BE THANKS - FULL	33
CHAPTER 3	MAKE PRAISE HAPPEN!	45
CHAPTER 4	WEAPONS OF PRAISE	57
BENEFITS OF PRAISE		63

PART II

Pray Until Something Happens

CHAPTER 5	POWER OF PRAYER	71
CHAPTER 6	THE PLACE OF FAITH	93
CHAPTER 7	RELEASE YOUR ANOINTING	103
CHAPTER 8	YOUR PATH TO VICTORY	119

PART III

Persist Until Something Happens

CHAPTER 9	POWER TO PERSIST AND PERSEVERE	129
CHAPTER 10	HAVING DONE ALL, STAND!	135

HISTORY MAKERS	141
BIBLIOGRAPHY	147
ACKNOWLEDGMENTS	149
ABOUT THE AUTHOR	151

INTRODUCTION

Blessed is the people that know the joyful sound: they shall walk, O LORD, in the light of thy countenance.

Psalm 89:15

Sometimes life and the pressures of this world can have you so low that getting up isn't even on your mind. You may be in a storm of life and all you see is darkness and you are crying out to God, "God, where are you? Lord, have you forgotten me? God, do you hear my prayer?" If you have not yet seen those dark sides of life or wondered if God is still near or is hearing your prayer, just keep on living because your day is right around the corner. But no matter how grim things may seem, no matter how dark the road may get, no matter how high are the hills that you have to climb, no matter what the judge says in that courtroom, no matter what the doctor says about that condition, *you still have a guarantee!*

When the children of Judah found themselves outnumbered by the hostile armies of Ammon, Moab, and Mount Seir, King Jehoshaphat and all the people sought the Lord for His help. The Lord assured the people that this would be *His* battle. He told them to go out against the enemies, and He would do the fighting for them. So what did the children of Judah do? Being people of "praise" who knew that God manifests His power through praise, they sent their army against their enemies—led by the praisers!

So, on they went ahead of the army declaring, "Praise the Lord, for His mercy endureth forever!" And the

Scripture says, "when they began to sing and to praise, the LORD set ambushments against the children of Ammon, Moab, and Mount Seir, which were come against Judah; and they were smitten" (2 Chronicles 20:22).

There is no situation you will ever face in your life—and I do mean *no* situation—that will take more than praise to defeat. Why? Because praise brings God into any situation, and no adversity, no enemy, can ever stop God. Here's how it works: When you *pray*, God answers; but when you *praise*, He steps in, in all His glory, might, power, and awesomeness. If you want to secure God's company in the midst of any conflict, situation, or circumstance, just release yourself to praise, and God will be there in person. When God shows up on the scene, every devil gives way. The Scripture says, *"Finally my brethren be strong in the Lord and in the power of His might"* (Ephesians 6:10). It is by His might that we have our strength, by the boundless might that He provides. In Him, we put on the whole armor of God, we put on the new man, we stand our ground, we persist—in our faith, in our thoughts, in our words, in our deeds, and in our lifestyles.

Yes, we *all* face challenges and difficult times. But God said: *"My plans for you are good and not evil, to give you a future and a hope"* (Jeremiah 29:11). God's plans for you are good, no matter what has happened in your past. His plans will always be for your good! God can turn your setbacks into fresh starts! He can take your tragedy and turn it into triumph! So let go of the past, seek God's plan, and develop that vision of victory for your life!

The Scripture says, *"he which hath begun a good work in you will perform it until the day of Jesus Christ"* (Philippians 1:6). God knows the suffering that we as believers go through. He sees all of our struggles each and every day. He knew about our suffering and our struggles before the foundation of this world. The Bible says that God "did foreknow" even before the foundation of the world (Romans 8:28-39).

God prompted me to write this book to inform you that He has commanded victory to be yours! And when God commands something, it is going to happen! When God commanded light to come, light came streaming in at 186,000 miles per second, and light is still coming! Our Father in heaven has commanded that we live in victory. That means that no matter what you are going through, no matter how dark it looks, you can be encouraged that the darkness has to give way to the light. Defeat has to give way to victory! But in order to open that door to victory, you must continually do what the psalmist did and *constantly praise His name*. Don't go around muttering about your problems; go around talking about your God! Don't go around speaking words of defeat and failure; speak words of faith and victory! Quit worrying and start worshipping! Start praising and thanking God and expect things to change in your favor.

My brothers and sisters, there is a highway of praise. It's a freeway in fact that keeps going from triumph to triumph, faith to faith, glory to glory, and victory to victory! As you read this book, open up to the light of God's word, which is able to bring about a forceful and positive turnaround in your present situation, no matter what it may be.

I believe this book will prepare you for a powerful spiritual encounter! You will be introduced to a new way of living – a life style of Praise, Prayer, and Persistence!

PART I

PRAISE UNTIL SOMETHING HAPPENS

CHAPTER 1

WHAT IS PRAISE?

Praise is appreciating God for His person. It is honoring God for His character, power, mercy, grace, knowledge, and healing. We offer praise to God in acknowledging His excellent being. In praise we just appreciate and worship Him for who He is.

Praise calms every storm; it soothes every pain. Praise gives courage to faint souls and raises the downtrodden. Praise sets on high those who have discovered the secrets of praising God both in good and in bad times. It is a beautiful thing to give God praise. It is comely to God (Psalm 147:1). Praise excites God. Praise motivates and mobilizes God. You can get to God easier through praise. David, the man after God's own heart, became God's darling by praise. God's heart was always with him. The whole of Saul's army could not handle David.

If you want God to back you up, here's the key: Live a life of endless praise. God will always be there. All those who seek your downfall will remain down and out while you keep rising.

Praise will build you up spiritually and keep you from crumbling, "for the joy of the LORD is your strength" (Nehemiah 8:10). The Apostle Paul, who was persecuted and suffered far more than most of us, put it all in perspective in 2 Corinthians 4:17-18: *"For our light affliction, which is but for a moment, is working for us a far more exceeding and eternal weight of glory, while we do not look at the things which are seen, but at the things which are not seen. For the things which are seen are temporary, but the things which are not seen are eternal."* First, Paul said that in light of eternity our affliction is just for a moment. He looked beyond the physical and into the spiritual realm. Praise will push you into the spiritual realm so you can see all that God has done for you. Paul and Silas praised God in prison.

"About midnight Paul and Silas were praying and singing hymns to God, and the other prisoners were listening to them. Suddenly there was such a violent earthquake that the foundations of the prison were shaken. At once all the prison doors flew open, and everybody's chains came loose."

Acts 16:25-26

The praise of Paul and Silas is what released the power of God and brought the earthquake that delivered them from their captivity!

If you want to see God back you up, live a life of endless praise

---

Did you know that the very best thing to do before you do anything else is to praise God? Have you ever been in a situation when you felt all alone? Or have you encountered a difficult situation in your life and didn't know what to do? Maybe you lost your job or suffered the loss of someone very close to your heart. How about the good times, such as when you received a raise from your boss or earned high marks in school or maybe even won an award? At such low and high moment what do you usually do? What is your first response?

Praising God makes every circumstance of our lives complete, essential, and eminently worthwhile. Praise does not merely affect us but is also a powerful weapon against the devil—a weapon that has no negative fallout. Jehoshaphat appointed singers to lead his army into battle with praise unto the Lord, and when they marched onto that battle singing and praising God the Lord God set an ambush and defeated their enemies.

My friend, I challenge you this very day to praise God and see if He will not cause your enemies to fear you! Begin to train your tongue to praise God and your heart to make a praiseful melody to Him! The power in praise and worship goes beyond all that you can imagine! When true praise goes up the blessings of God rain down. With praise we can breakthrough and have smooth ride to victory on the journey of life.

The power of praise has no limitations

HIS BENEFITS

PRAISE BRINGS DELIVERANCE AND FREEDOM

"And when they had laid many stripes upon them, they cast them into prison, charging the jailor to keep them safely: Who, having received such a charge, thrust them into the inner prison, and made their feet fast in the stocks. And at midnight Paul and Silas prayed, and sang praises unto God: and the prisoners heard them. And suddenly there was a great earthquake, so that the foundations of the prison were shaken: and immediately all the doors were opened, and every one's bands were loosed."

Acts 16:23-27

The Scriptures tell us that God inhabits the praise of His people. Although prayer is good and very powerful, God responds to praise in a special way, different from the way He responds to our merely asking in prayers. The praises flowing from through the mouths of Paul and Silas within the four walls of that prison so caught the attention of Almighty God that He did not send an angel to deliver them as did He at other times when the brethren only prayed! He literally shook the doors open and loosed the prisoners' bonds! It is astounding and so comforting to know that God responds to the praises of men, especially when those praises flow from pure hearts and undefiled lips.

The power of praise has no limitations, especially offered genuinely from a pure heart in a difficult situation (that is, a situation that does not seem to lend itself to rejoicing or excitement). The surest way to get Almighty God committed in any situation is to praise Him and praise Him and praise Him and praise Him! God is bigger than all our problems and challenges put together! So when we come into His presence, the most important thing is not emphasizing our problems at the expense of offering Him the sincere praise that is due to His name forever.

God is awesome and far bigger than the power of language can ever describe, so our praise of Him is not only about the good and wonderful things we say about Him, but about the condition of our hearts. We can live a victorious life and reap harvests of sweat-less breakthroughs when we praise God in the midst of seemingly hopeless situations and raging storms.

PRAISE CAUSES OUR ENEMIES TO FLEE BEFORE US

"And Jehoshaphat stood in the congregation of Judah and Jerusalem, in the house of the LORD, before the new court,

What is Praise?

And said, O LORD God of our fathers, art not thou God in heaven? and rulest not thou over all the kingdoms of the heathen? and in thine hand is there not power and might, so that none is able to withstand thee? Art not thou our God, who didst drive out the inhabitants of this land before thy people Israel, and gavest it to the seed of Abraham thy friend for ever? And they dwelt therein, and have built thee a sanctuary therein for thy name, saying, If, when evil cometh upon us, as the sword, judgment, or pestilence, or famine, we stand before this house, and in thy presence, (for thy name is in this house,) and cry unto thee in our affliction, then thou wilt hear and help. And now, behold, the children of Ammon and Moab and mount Seir, whom thou wouldest not let Israel invade, when they came out of the land of Egypt, but they turned from them, and destroyed them not; Behold, I say, how they reward us, to come to cast us out of thy possession, which thou hast given us to inherit. O our God, wilt thou not judge them? for we have no might against this great company that cometh against us; neither know we what to do: but our eyes are upon thee. And all Judah stood before the LORD, with their little ones, their wives, and their children. Then upon Jahaziel the son of Zechariah, the son of Benaiah, the son of Jeiel, the son of Mattaniah, a Levite of the sons of Asaph, came the Spirit of the LORD in the midst of the congregation; And he said, Hearken ye, all Judah, and ye inhabitants of Jerusalem, and thou king Jehoshaphat, Thus saith the LORD unto you, Be not afraid nor dismayed by reason of this great multitude; for the battle is not yours, but God's. To morrow go ye down against them: behold, they come up by the cliff of Ziz; and ye shall find them at the end of the brook, before the wilderness of Jeruel. Ye shall not need to fight in this battle: set yourselves, stand ye still, and see the salvation of the LORD with you, O Judah and Jerusalem: fear not, nor be dismayed; to morrow go out against them: for the LORD will be with you."

2 Chronicles 20:5-17

In 2 Chronicles 20, enemies were coming against the people of God and Jehoshaphat was afraid and said, *"We have no power against this great multitude that is coming against us; nor do we know what to do, but our eyes are upon You."* In much the same way, if you are in Christ you can be sure that you are going to be opposed on every side. May you never minimize or forget that. Jehoshaphat and Israel were facing a physical battle, but a spiritual battle was also going on, and all of that is a picture of the spiritual battle in which we believers are engaged today.

Do not be afraid nor dismayed

We are living in a realm of unseen powers and principalities (Ephesians 6). The devil is Christ's adversary and thus also the adversary of all who are in Christ. The devil and his angels are on a relentless quest to tear down the work of Jesus Christ. Never forget that because you are Christ's workmanship and the Church is His new creation, so you are target of the evil one. The enemy, the devil is prowling around like a roaring lion, seeking whom he may devour (1 Peter 5:8). He and his (fallen) angels are working to do all they can to wreak havoc in the lives of the people of God. Of course, we know that they are still under the sovereign hand of God, which limits their activities.

From a human perspective, did it really make much sense for Jehoshaphat to take that time to fast and pray or spend time worshiping the Lord before and during the battle? Before you answers, consider that there were not a few, not even a multitude, but a *great multitude* of armies coming to battle. So, *No!* Jehoshaphat actions make no sense if we look at them merely through human, secular eyes. Too many Christians think that they should praise God when everything is okay and pray only for the little things, but when it comes to the really big things (like those great multitudes), well, they really need to help God out a bit or more! *How ridiculous!* Would that our long-suffering God might grant them patience to trust Him and wait upon Him rather than resort to their own schemes and rely on their pitiful resources.

We must understand that God's ways and God's thoughts are higher than ours. Whenever we humble ourselves and seek God's face and heavenly wisdom in prayer and fasting, and when we give Him the due reverence He deserves and demands—no matter how foolish and weak that may seem in the eyes of men, we can trust that God will never fail to bless us and strengthen us and provide for all of our needs for doing His will.

PRAISE SETS AN ATMOSPHERE FOR OUR HEARING FROM GOD

When you find yourself needing to hear from God, you must begin worshiping. In an atmosphere of praise we begin hearing from God. We see this to be the case in the Antioch church.

"As they ministered to the Lord, and fasted, the Holy Ghost said, Separate me Barnabas and Saul for the work whereunto I have called them."

Acts 13:2

The Bible says, *"As they ministered to the Lord, and fasted, the Holy Ghost said...."* Notice that it was while they were engaged in ministering to the Lord the Holy Spirit spoke to the church saying, *"Set apart for Me Barnabas and Saul for he work to which I have called them'* (NASB). I have found that when I am in those services where praise and worship are the most intense I sense the greatest anointing in my ministering—whether singing, preaching, or teaching. God seems to speak the clearest in this type of atmosphere. The sound of heaven comes through praise and worship. Whether in our personal time with God or in a public setting, praise is the key to our hearing the voice of God.

We find this is true when we are in a spiritual battle as well. During those times when we are going through difficulty and spiritual conflict we most desperately need to hear from God. Ahab and Jehoshaphat were going to battle with Moab when they ran out of water. They were perplexed as to what to do and afraid they were being led to defeat.

"Jehoshaphat said, is there not here a prophet of the LORD, that we may inquire of the LORD by him? And one of the king of Israel's servants answered and said, here is Elisha the son of Shaphat, which poured water on the hands of Elijah. And Jehoshaphat said, the word of the LORD is with him."

2 Kings 3:11-12

They went to Elisha to get a word from God, and one of the first things Elisha said was: *"But now bring me a minstrel (musician). And it came to pass, when the minstrel played, that the hand of the LORD came upon him* (2 Kings 3:15). He said, *"Thus says the LORD."* When the musician began to play the Lord spoke to Elisha and gave him the needed Word to lead them to victory. Elisha knew that worship was a necessary factor for him to hear from God. As a worship minister this shows me how very important the worship leader's job is.

Those who minister on a worship team must never underestimate the importance of their calling. You are the ones who set an atmosphere for the church to hear God speak!

We can notice that, *"When the minstrel played, that the hand of the LORD came upon him* [Elisha]." Worship ushers in the anointing of God. Ministers of the Word simply do not realize how dependent they are on the worship leaders. This is why praise and worship are so imperative to any church service, to any meeting where the Word is going to be preached, and even to our personal time with the Lord. If you want to see a mighty move of God in your life, you should always have a time of praise and worship prior to your study of the Word, whether it's in a corporate setting or in your own personal devotions.

PRAISE RELEASES THE GENEROSITY OF GOD

Think about your children coming to you and telling you how wonderful and great you are. Your immediate response is usually to say, "Okay, you're buttering me up. So what do you want?" You laugh and wait for the answer. But if they are *constantly* praising you, you are apt to give them anything they desire. God responds the same way to His children—us! If you are continually praising and worshiping the Lord, telling Him how much you love Him and how great He is, He is likely to give you anything you desire, sometimes before you even ask.

In the book of Isaiah, the Lord says:

"It shall come to pass that before they call, I will answer; And while they are still speaking, I will hear."

Isaiah 65:24

How great is that! Praise brings this to fulfillment in our lives. If you spend more time in praise and worship, you will have a lot less to pray about.

Praise Releases Stress and Anxiety

"Be anxious for nothing, but in everything by prayer and supplication, with thanksgiving, let your requests be made known to God; and the peace of God, which surpasses all understanding, will guard your hearts and minds through Christ Jesus."

Philippians 4:6-7

The three-fold prescription for stress and anxiety is: Prayer, Praise, and Positive mindset (read Philippians 4:8). I will share with you how these three work together in Parts II and III of this book.

Praise sets an atmosphere for us to hear from God

In Word of God says that we are to bring our problems to the Lord in prayer— *"casting all your care upon Him, for He cares for you"* (1 Peter 5:7). You might be surprised to hear me say that *prayer alone is not enough.* Prayer focuses on the problem whereas praise focuses us on the solution. Prayer keeps our concentration on the cause of our stress and anxiety. It is important to pray, indeed, but we dare not stop there. We must move from prayer to praise so that we do not dwell on the problem but on the solution— thanking Him for the answer.

PRAISE IS A LIFESTYLE

"Blessed is the people that know the joyful sound: they shall walk, O LORD, in the light of thy countenance."

Psalms 89:15

All too often, praising God is something that we leave at church, as though praise is something that happens only when we come together with other Christians. That is a lie of the enemy because praise should be a vital part of a believer's lifestyle, intermingled with their daily prayer life. At work, in the car, at home in bed, in class at school, on the Internet, or anywhere else: Praising the Lord brings the refreshing of the Lord's presence, along with His power and anointing.

"...I will bless the LORD at all times: his praise shall continually be in my mouth."

Psalms 34:1

Praise is an expression of faith and a declaration of victory! It declares that we believe that God is with us and is in control of the outcome of every single circumstance and situation we face in life (Romans 8:28). Praise is a "sacrifice," something that we offer to God sacrificially, not just because we feel like it but because we believe in Him and wish to please Him.

"Therefore by Him let us continually offer the sacrifice of praise to God, that is, the fruit of our lips, giving thanks to His name."

Hebrews 13:15

Praising God involves many actions—verbal expressions of adoration and thanksgiving, singing, playing instruments, shouting, dancing, lifting or clapping our hands. True praise, however, is not merely *going through these motions*. Jesus spoke about the hypocrisy of the Pharisees, whose worship was only an outward show and not from the heart.

"These people draw near to Me with their mouth, And honor Me with their lips, But their heart is far from Me."

Matthew 15:8

Genuine praising of God is a matter of humility and sincere devotion to the Lord from *within*.

Praise calms every storm

THE PLACE OF WORSHIP

"But the hour cometh, and now is, when the true worshippers shall worship the Father in spirit and in truth: for the Father seeketh such to worship him."

John 4:23

God is a spirit and they that worship Him must worship Him in spirit and in truth. It doesn't say that we can worship God anyway we want! Rather, "must worship Him in spirit and in truth." The word *must* makes it absolute. No other way of worshipping God is acceptable to Him. According to *Webster's Dictionary*, the word "must" expresses "an obligation, a requirement, a necessity, a certainty, and something that must be done." When the word "must" is used it means that it is not optional but mandatory. In the passage above the word "must" is expressing the *only acceptable way* to worship God is in spirit and in truth.

Worshipping God in spirit and in truth is a serious matter that we must not take lightly. For your own soul's sake, make sure that you are worshipping God in spirit and in truth. True worship is a heartfelt expression of love, adoration, admiration, fascination, wonder, and celebration. It is something that happens in your heart and soul when you begin to praise God for who He is and thank Him for what He has done. It cannot be ritualistic. It cannot be just an external act of going through the motions.

Too many Christians today believe that worshipping God means going to church and singing songs. Singing worship songs is one way to worship God, but it is not what the Apostle Paul talks about in Romans 12:1:

"I beseech you therefore, brethren, by the mercies of God, that ye present your bodies a living sacrifice, holy, acceptable unto God, which is your reasonable service."

The purpose of our worship is to glorify, honor, praise, exalt, and please God. Our worship must express our sincere adoration and loyalty to God for His grace—His gracious gift of salvation that provides us with the way to escape the bondage and ultimate penalty of sin—eternal death. The nature of the worship God demands is the prostration of our souls before Him in humble and contrite submission.

True worship is a heartfelt expression of love, adoration, admiration, fascination, wonder, and celebration

---

Worship is a time when we pay deep, sincere, and awesome respect, love, and fear to the One who created us. It is that secret place where we develop a lifestyle of reverence and gratitude to God.

Worship is not difficult; in fact, it comes natural to us because every human being—Christian or non-Christian, pagan or holy—was designed to worship. Not only were we designed to worship, but every person who has ever lived (now or in the past) does in fact worship ... *something*. Consider a group of sports fans watching and talking about a "big" game. They worship. Consider a group of teenagers at that "hot" band's concert. They worship. People readily worship food, sports, arts, and music. Some worship comfort, control, power, achievement, work, money, and relationships, but God calls all of us—that includes you and me—to worship Him.

He commands it, He desires it, He pursues it, He deserves it, and He will reward it. For God bestows His provision, grace, sovereignty, and power on those who worship Him in spirit and in truth. But know this: Even if you choose not to worship God, you are worshipping something else. And whether you worship a job, achievement, money, or a person, you are doing so to your detriment. Why? Because at some point the object of your worship will fail to come through for you.

Acts 17:24-25 says:

"God that made the world and all things therein, seeing that he is Lord of heaven and earth, dwelleth not in temples made with hands; Neither is worshipped with men's hands, as though he needed any thing, seeing he giveth to all life, and breath, and all things."

True worship will cause you to reflect on the majesty and graciousness of God and Christ, contrasted with your own unworthiness. God does not *need* your worship, but you must worship Him to please Him. Your singing, praying, studying His word, giving, and communion are designed by God to bring you closer to Him and to cause you to think more like He thinks and thus to become more like Him.

"Draw near to God and He will draw near to you."

James 4:8 (ESV)

Your worship is a weapon. It is not only honors and magnifies God but also edifies you (builds you up) and strengthens you. Worship helps you develop a God-like and Christ-like character. You become like those you admire and worship. When you worship God you tend to value what God values and gradually take on the characteristics and qualities of God. You develop such traits as forgiveness, tenderness, justice, righteousness, purity, kindness, and love. All of this is preparing you for eternal life in heaven with the Father.

If you choose not to worship God, you need to understand that you are worshipping something else

---

Something really happens when we find ourselves in the place of worship. Let us take a look at the worship experience of one of God's prophets recorded in Isaiah 6:1-4 (NIV).

"In the year that King Uzziah died, I saw the Lord seated on a throne, high and exalted, and the train of his robe filled the temple. Above him were seraphs, each with six wings: With two wings they covered their faces, with two they covered their feet, and with two they were flying. And they were calling to one another: 'Holy, holy, holy is the LORD Almighty; the whole earth is full of his glory.' At the sound of their voices the doorposts and thresholds shook and the temple was filled with smoke."

When you are in this level of adoration, worship will bring you two things:

First, it brings an **Upward Look**, a glance at God on His throne in all His glory. It refocuses your view of God. It pulls your affections off your idols and puts them onto God. It causes you to remember how good He is, how big, kind, powerful, and loving He is, and how holy He is.

Second, worship brings an **Inward Look**. Isaiah 6:5-7 says:

"Woe to me!' I cried. 'I am ruined! For I am a man of unclean lips, and I live among a people of unclean lips, and my eyes have seen the King, the LORD Almighty.' Then one of the seraphs flew to me with a live coal in his hand, which he had taken with tongs from the altar. With it he touched my mouth and said, 'See, this has touched your lips; your guilt is taken away and your sin atoned for."

The purpose of our worship is to glorify, honor, praise, exalt, and please God

---

When you see God for who He really is, as Isaiah did, you start to see yourself for who you really are. You start seeing things in your heart and in your life that really didn't bother you before. But notice that after Isaiah saw and confessed his sinfulness, he also experienced the mercy, grace, and forgiveness of God. That's what happens when you really worship.

Unpretentious praise and worship pleases the Lord. He delights in the love and devotion of His children. According to the Scriptures, the various expressions of praise bring blessing to the Lord. He eagerly awaits the fragrance of our affections, desiring to manifest His sweet presence and power in our midst. *"...the true worshipers shall worship the Father in spirit and in truth: for the Father seeketh such to worship him"* (John 4:23).

Simple obedience to the law of praise will hook you on to the miraculous line of life.

CHAPTER 2

BE THANKS - FULL

To be 'thanks-full' is what makes praise genuine. The more thankful you are, the more you will find there is to be thankful for. A person cannot be complaining and be praiseful at the same time. You must be thankful before you can be joyful, and you must be joyful before you can sing, lest your song become mere noise.

If you are not giving thanks to God and praising Him you do not know what you are missing. *God inhabits the praise of His people.* And the Bible says that it is a good thing to give thanks to Him. That means it is a bad thing to be unthankful.

"In every thing give thanks: for this is the will of God in Christ Jesus concerning you."

1 Thessalonians 5:18

If you are thoughtful, you will discover that there is always something to thank God for. Thanksgiving is an attitude of appreciation and gratitude to God for something that He has given you or for what He has done. In heaven's protocol, thanksgiving precedes praise. Only a thankful heart can be praiseful. One of the great commandments is to give thanksgiving to God for all that He has done for us. In Psalm 100:4 we are taught to *"enter into his gates with thanksgiving, and into his courts with praise: be thankful unto him, and bless his name."* Christ, the Master himself, was the perfect example of obeying this commandment.

"And Jesus took the loaves; and when he had given thanks, he distributed to the disciples, and the disciples to them that were set down; and likewise of the fishes as much as they would."

John 6:11

In fact, this is not the only time we see God the Son giving thanks to God the Father. Another instance is when Jesus established the Lord's Supper. In Luke 22 we are told that before passing the bread around at the Last Supper Jesus took the loaf and gave thanks. Thanksgiving is one of the major secrets of life! It establishes your blessings as permanent features of your life. It grants you access to the hurt-free zone of life.

Only a thankful heart can be praiseful

The Bible teaches that a thankful attitude joins heaven and earth, whereas an ungrateful attitude keeps heaven and earth—the spiritual and the material realms—separate. When we are thankful, we recognize that food, shelter, and all other necessities come to us from the mercy of Almighty God. Thankfulness turns our hearts towards heaven. Thankfulness is one of the things that lifts us above the level of beasts.

"And let the peace of God rule in your hearts, to the which also ye are called in one body; and be ye thankful. Let the word of Christ dwell in you richly in all wisdom; teaching and admonishing one another in psalms and hymns and spiritual songs, singing with grace in your hearts to the Lord. And whatsoever ye do in word or deed, do all in the name of the Lord Jesus, giving thanks to God and the Father by him."

Colossians 3:15-17

If you want to recover what is lost, give thanks to God! If anything is not working in your life, just give thanks! This is a special honor from God. It will put an end to all complaining and murmuring. When thanksgiving becomes the order of the day in your life, your life will have taste and it will have order. You will live an enviable, resourceful life. People will see Jesus in your life. A life of thanksgiving is a life of sweat-less and tasteful Christian experience. It is sweet! It is of God! Jesus lived a practical life of thanksgiving and He never lacked.

Learn to focus on the past acts of God to get your present needs met

Learn to focus on the past acts of God to get your present needs met. Take your eyes off of your needs and focus them on God. Thank Him, if not what He has done in your own life, at least for what you have heard that He did in someone else's life. What He has done is living proof that He is bigger than your need. If you will settle down to acknowledge Him, *He* will acknowledge *you*.

GIVE THANKS FOR ALL THINGS

"So they departed from the presence of the council, rejoicing that they were counted worthy to suffer shame for His name. And daily in the temple, and in every house, they did not cease teaching and preaching Jesus as the Christ."

Acts 5:40-41

We are to be thankful for all things—negative experiences as well as positive experiences, in sickness and in health, in poverty and in wealth, in prison and in freedom, when we are loved by people and when they hate us. In Acts 5 we read that the apostles were flogged for their obedience to Jesus Christ's command to preach the gospel. When you know that all things work together for good to those who love God, to those who are the called according to His purpose (Romans 8:28), you walk in peace, convinced that the Sovereign Lord of the universe redeems all experiences for your good, especially the negative experiences of suffering.

In Psalm 119, we see that the writer profited from his negative experiences: *"Before I was afflicted I went astray, But now I keep Your word"* (v. 67). I am sure that this man did not want to be afflicted, but he understood the power of thanksgiving and its benefits. God does not check with us! He does what He pleases for our good. There is a level of glory in you that exposes itself only as you go through crushing experiences. Can you stand to be blessed?

In verse 71-75, he says:

"It is good for me that I have been afflicted, That I may learn Your statutes. The law of Your mouth is better to me Than thousands of coins of gold and silver. Your hands have made me and fashioned me; Give me understanding, that I may learn Your commandments. Those who fear You will be glad when they see me, Because I have hoped in Your word. I know, O LORD, that Your judgments are right, And that in faithfulness You have afflicted me."

There is a shift in the atmosphere when you give thanks to God, no matter how severe and threatening the storm may be. The God of your tight places says, "My Grace is sufficient for you" (2 Corinthians 12:9). "I AM always enough." Always enough when you have nothing! Always enough to heal you! I AM always enough to deliver you, always enough to fix that problem, to get you out of that situation! I AM always enough for whatever you need! Hallelujah! God can't really get the glory out of your life until you stop relying on things that don't work. His grace is sufficient. Give Him praise through your thanksgiving and you will see the hands of the Lord doing mighty work in your life.

Learn to focus on the past acts of God to get your present needs met

---

DON'T FORGET HIS GOODNESS

"Through the LORD's mercies we are not consumed, Because His compassions fail not. They are new every morning; 'Great is Your faithfulness. The LORD is my portion,' says my soul."

Lamentations 3:22-24

God has been faithful and He always will be. Even when we lack faith, He remains faithful. The Bible says, *"Great is His faithfulness, and His mercies are new every morning"* (Lamentations 3:23). Every day God's thoughts toward us are so numerous that they cannot even be counted. So already you have more things to be thankful for than you can even name or count. You have every spiritual blessing in the heavenly places in Christ Jesus. Eternity in paradise with God is yours. When all else fails, God never fails, and His mercy, love, and kindness endure forever!

Friend, there is so much to be thankful for, and so many blessings to count. In fact, if only you could see all that God does, you would see that you have more mercies than you could ever account for. Don't let the missiles of the devil knock you down such that you forget that you have Christ and the many blessings of God. If you want to see the benefits of thanksgiving, then you should *never lose hope because you always have reason to be thankful.*

I have included some testimonies of ordinary men and women like you, who believed God's Word and applied it! They not only experienced divine providence in their situations but also a supernatural turnaround!

"But I will hope continually, And will praise You yet more and more. My mouth shall tell of Your righteousness And Your salvation all the day, For I do not know their limits."

Psalm 71:14-15

Testimonies

"I really don't know where to begin, but here it goes... all my life from when I was a child all the way till I was 41, I never had the love that I knew I could've had. I came from a broken home; my grandparents raised me and my brother. They provided the material things we needed, but not the love we needed. It's not their fault; they tried. I grew up with a lot of anger inside me, never knew how to love any one person, had a very hard heart, and would not allow anyone or anything in. I had lost and basically given my life to the devil of this world, but one day my wife told me she wanted a divorce, and I felt so unloved again. I didn't know how to handle it, but God grabbed me and said to me, NOT THIS TIME, YOU'RE MINE AND YOU ARE NOT GOING DOWN THAT ROAD AGAIN. Since then I've surrendered myself to God, and He has taught me how to love, care, speak, feel, and has been putting people around me in my church to help me grow in

Him so that now I have so much love and a soft heart. I feel for everything as though it was mine from the beginning."It took me 41 years to find the peace in my life and all I can do is thank God for His Son Jesus Christ, for the blood He shed for my sins. Thank Him for my church and my Pastor. If it wasn't for God grabbing me and telling me that, I probably would not be here today. All I ever wanted to do was die so I wouldn't feel the pain that was inside of me all my life, but God didn't let me go this time, and I am SO THANKFUL. I feel like an awesome person, and reading His Word every day I get great comfort from Him. I finally have the peace and His love that I know is so true, and I know that if it wasn't for God, I wouldn't be going to spend eternity with the people that I care or love so much in my life. THANK YOU, GOD!"

- J.J

There is a shift in the atmosphere when you give thanks to God

---

"I wanted to share a testimony with anyone who may read this, so that you, too, can see that God is a great God. Every week I get paid and before anything else, I always make sure to tithe and give 10% of what I make that week to the Lord. And before I do I always pray over it and ask God to always provide for me, and He always does. His Word says ask in My Name and you shall receive what you ask for and God cannot lie. Here is a perfect example of His love for me: It was income tax time and I didn't think I was going to get very much money back from taxes but I HAD HIGH EXPECTANCY!!! Something inside of me told me there was going to be more. I kept speaking there was going to be more, but some people doubted it. When I went to get my taxes done, the man put my information in the computer and he looked at me and said,

'Guess what? I got you more money back,' and I looked at him with a big smile and I said, 'Are you serious?' And he said, 'Yes' and then typed more things into the computer and he said, 'I got you even more money back.' I didn't really say much after that because I was speechless. All I kept doing was thanking God. I just felt so blessed and happy, so after we were all done I ended up leaving with three times more than what I thought I would get back. This is a perfect example of what God can do. The Lord is able to do immeasurably more than all we ask or imagine. He is a great God, and I knew in my heart that there was going to be something bigger when I walked in there, and I never once doubted that. Always remember to put God first, remain in Him, and He will remain in you. And He will never let you down."

- **Karinna**

God grabbed me and said to me, NOT THIS TIME, YOU'RE MINE AND YOU ARE NOT GOING DOWN THAT ROAD AGAIN

"Eleven years ago, I went in to my dermatologist for a check up. Having grown up in the sun all summer on the coast I had had some skin cancer problems. At this visit he saw a growth on my leg and did a biopsy. He stated I needed to have it operated on immediately. I told him it would have to wait as we were going to a Renewal conference that we usually went to and then I was going to spend several weeks with my grandchildren. He said, 'I do not recommend you waiting.' I did anyway. At the conference I did ask for prayer, as usual, but not specific. The Monday we got back I went into the doctor for the operation. He looked at it and said it looked different and asked if I had done that prayer thing. I said yes. He operated and found nothing but scar tissue from the biopsy. I later found out that this had been a Stage 4 melanoma. I should have died from it. The very best part of this story is that the doctor became a believer and came to Jesus as a result of it. His wife had been trying for years to get him churched and he resisted. God is so good when He uses us that way."

- J. John

I AM always enough

"This past year has been a year of battles. Satan has attacked me in every way he could...finances, love, family, friends, and work. I praise God our Heavenly Father for protecting me and supplying me with wisdom, grace, guidance, and peace to overcome these attacks. Right now, I am seeing victory on every front, and it is because of our Lord and Savior's mighty power. Praise be to God in the name of Jesus."

- Tasha

God does not check with us! He does what He pleases for our good

"I was one of those people Sunday who was feeling a wave of emotions (and I know better). My husband's job had cut his hours back last year, which caused us to get behind in some things, especially our property taxes. There is money that we are owed from several sources but it has been one delay after another and the Township has been less than sympathetic. My husband has not wanted to deal with this issue at all saying if they sell the house, so be it. I have been standing for both of us. The tax sale is scheduled for June 29th. After Sunday when I really gave it all to Daddy (God), I purposed in my heart not to think about it again. I just began to praise Him and put

Him in remembrance of all of those things that have been prophesied at the same time confessing His word over everything. I told Him that I didn't need to know how He would work it out and that I knew He had me regardless. I have been in that area of 'perfect peace' resting in Him knowing if I had to walk away from it all, He still had me and would provide for me. Still making calls about the money owed to us, I finally rested in that as well and really didn't care whether it came in or not just trusting and praising Daddy (God). I knew in my spirit that something had shifted in my situation and I began to praise Him in a different way. "Weeks later, my youngest son got a refund check from college and it is for almost exactly the amount that I need to cover the Property Taxes. This doesn't even take into account the other funds that I am waiting to receive. That day was when He (God) placed very strongly in my spirit that He had taken care of everything. I deposited the check on the next day. Hallelujah!...

"Another testimony for someone I have been mentoring and interceding for a breakthrough: My friend 'C' told me that God was about to do something miraculous in the life a young lady I had been praying for and mentoring. I didn't know who at the time because I intercede for so many people... This young lady posted a message on her Facebook that had me concerned. It was a cry to Daddy (God) for help. As I prayed, He had me contact her. Within 20 minutes of the prayer (she had a financial need), I shared with her what Daddy (God) had said about her. She checked her account and found that there was a deposit that she was not expecting that took care of that need. Breakthrough again! Daddy (God) also said that the breakthroughs in people's lives are going to be like a chain reaction for those who are ready to receive. Hallelujah!"

Blessings,

- L.K.

"Oh, give thanks to the LORD, for He is good! For His mercy endures forever."

Psalm 107:1

CHAPTER 3

MAKE PRAISE HAPPEN!

"Let the people praise thee, O God; let all the people praise thee."

Psalm 67:3

No matter what's happening —whether you are having low moments or high moments—your focus must stay on God. You are the one to make praise happen; praising God starts with you! Your situation should *never* dictate your faith and confession. The word "let" in the passage above implies this. Do you want a way out of that difficult situation? Then you have to let praise happen! Let gladness happen (verse 4). Why? Because if you have lost anything at all, He is the reason why you did not lose *everything*. This is certainly the message of the psalmist:

"I will bless the LORD at all times: his praise shall continually be in my mouth."

Psalm 34:1

In other words, God is worthy of your praise in the best of times, in the worst of times, and in all the mundane moments in between. In the early days of our ministry, whenever my car broke down or there was not enough money to pay bills, I would say, "Thank God, it is the *car* that broke down, not me," and "Thank You, Lord, for you are the great provider."

You don't wait for joy to come.... You make it happen. The psalmist said: *"I will praise the name of God with a song, and will magnify him with thanksgiving"* (Psalm 69:30). Many have been waiting for gladness to come into their lives all this while and have died under depression. They failed to realize what the psalmist meant when he said: *"I will praise...."* He meant this: *Praise is a conscious act of the will, not something you just stumble into.*

Your situation should never dictate your faith and confession

---

In the Scriptures we read about Paul and Silas, who were suffering one of life's low moments. For many days they had been stalked by a slave girl who had a spirit that enabled her to tell fortunes. Day after day she had shouted, *"These men are the servants of the most high God, which shew unto us the way of salvation"* (Acts 16:17b). Finally, Paul had heard enough of this and in the name of Jesus he commanded the spirit to leave the girl... which it did. The slave girl's owners, incensed by their loss of income, then stirred up the crowd and the leaders of the city to such a point that they stripped Paul and Silas, beat them, and threw them into jail and placed their feet in bonds.

What would most of us have done in such circumstances? Rejoiced? Praised God? Thanked Him for the blessing of persecution? No! Most of us would have moaned and groaned and grumbled "woe is me" about how unfair the people were and how unjustly we had been treated. What did Paul and Silas do? They didn't start complaining about the darkness or the stench of urine in the hole they had been thrown into. Instead, Paul said, "Silas, let's sing. Let's make praise happen!" So they spent the night praying and singing to the Lord—and not in a quiet, subdued manner, either. Their praise and worship was loud enough for the other prisoners to hear it. You are the one to generate joy around you!

David commanded his soul to bless the Lord at all times. *"Bless the LORD, O my soul: and all that is within me, bless his holy name"* (Psalm 103:1). In other words, he talked to himself—to his will, his emotions, and his intellect. Therefore, if you do as David did and command your soul to praise God, in reality you are commanding your body to obey the instructions it receives from your will, emotions, and intellect because your soul is your whole self (see Genesis 2:7).

You must develop an attitude in which praise becomes your protection all the time as you bring God around you. So whether you are at work, at school, at home cooking, on a bus or in the subway, taking care of children, playing with friends ... just make praise happen and keep making a sweet melody to the Lord. Choose to praise—because the choice is always yours. Make a choice that whatever you are going to do throughout the whole day, you are going to do with God! Don't wait for something special to happen. Instead, make sure that God is with you through your praise, and as you keep that joyful noise within you He will be there to handle everything.

When you are intoxicated with joy, it explodes in praise. Friend, if you can't be thankful for what you have received, be thankful for what God allowed you to escape (because you could always have suffered much worse)!

IN THE MIDST OF ALL GENERATE JOY

"Make a joyful noise unto the LORD, all ye lands. Serve the LORD with gladness: come before his presence with singing."

Psalm 100:1-2

Joy is the reward for victory over fear, depression, and all manner of sin. As a worship leader, I recognize clearly that without God you can do nothing and that without joy you can't have Him; so you must give yourself what it takes to maintain a heart full of joy. A joyless person should never expect a divine intervention in the storm of his or her life. The Bible says we should continue rejoicing in the Lord *at all times*.

"Rejoice in the Lord always: and again I say, Rejoice."

Philippians 4:4

As Christians, our hearts should be filled at all times to overflowing with thanksgiving to the God who created and redeemed us! Lovers praise their beloved, readers praise their favorite book, food-lovers praise their dish of choice, and we the Sons of God love to praise the things we enjoy because praise is not just the expression of that joy but also the completion of it. Our praise of God must overflow from our joy in God. To praise God is to enjoy Him to the fullest.

Don't wait for joy to come; make it happen

"And the angel said unto them, Fear not: for, behold, I bring you good tidings of great joy, which shall be to all people. For unto you is born this day in the city of David a Saviour, which is Christ the Lord."

Luke 2:10-11

The coming of Christ was proclaimed as the coming of joy to the world. So when Jesus steps into any life, that life becomes an embodiment of good tidings and great joy, because He is heaven's greatest deposit of joy. Christ is the genuine fountain of joy for mankind. That is why the happiest people in the world are believers. I believe strongly that if anyone cannot find joy in Christ, he can never find it anywhere else.

Joy is the reward for victory over fear, depression, and all manner of sin

---

CELEBRATE GOD WITH ALL YOUR HEART

"Praise ye the LORD. I will praise the LORD with my whole heart, in the assembly of the upright, and in the congregation."

Psalm 111:1

Provoke God to come down in the midst of your praise by worshipping and celebrating Him from a heart full of joy. It doesn't matter what is happening around you. God *always* has the final say. If hard times hit, God can still bless you in a greater way! In fact, when you learn to celebrate Him beyond your reality He will bless you beyond your dreams.

RELEASE YOUR FAITH

"And Jesus answering saith unto them, Have faith in God. For verily I say unto you, That whosoever shall say unto this mountain, Be thou removed, and be thou cast into the sea; and shall not doubt in his heart, but shall believe that those things which he saith shall come to pass; he shall have whatsoever he saith. Therefore I say unto you, What

things soever ye desire, when ye pray, believe that ye receive them, and ye shall have them."

Mark 11:22-24

In this passage, Jesus tells us how to release our faith. He said to the disciples, *"Have faith in God."* What word has the enemy spoken to you that has left you dismayed and greatly afraid? Listen to this: Saul's army sized up Goliath and felt small, but David sized up the Living God and knew that Goliath didn't stand a chance! When he began talking all that trash, David knew it was time to take out the garbage!!! God is saying, "You are relying on everyone and everything but Me—God. I will show you how to conquer your enemies and how to come out of this situation if you will simply trust Me."

Faith is necessary for every mountain to be moved. So it is time for you to release your faith and watch mountains move, hearts shift, and lives be changed around you.

HAVE AN ATTITUDE OF GRATITUDE

"Let no foul or polluting language come out of your mouth."

Ephesians 4:29

Your words can pollute or purify. If you constantly complain, you release poison into your life. Complaining is based not on your circumstances but on the attitude of your heart. If you keep the right attitude during your time of adversity, God will honor you.

When your heart is full of gratitude, there is no room for complaining. There is always something to thank God for, no matter what kind of adversity you have in your life. Start by thanking Him for giving you life and salvation through Jesus Christ. Thank Him for the air you breathe and the sunsets you enjoy. Thank Him for the promise in His Word that no matter where you are in life, He is leading, guiding, and prospering you.

Decide today to live a life of thanksgiving. Don't allow the poison of complaining to prevent you from receiving all that God has for you!

BE JOYFUL ALWAYS

"... For the joy of the Lord is your strength."
Nehemiah 8:10

David said, *"I will bless the Lord at all times. His praise shall continually be in my mouth"* (Psalm 34:1). *At all times* means in the good times as well as in the tough times, in the happy times as well as in the sad times. The Bible tells us to stay full of joy no matter what we are facing.

The joy of the Lord is our source of strength, and the enemy knows it. The enemy knows if he can get you down and discouraged that before long you will be weak and feeble and then he will be able to defeat you easily. When you are full of joy and have a good attitude, you keep yourself strong. That positive attitude of faith paves the way for God to work miracles in your life. It paves the way for God to turn your situation around!

Decide today to have a good attitude. Keep yourself full of His joy by meditating on the goodness and the promises of God. Be full of the joy of the Lord! If you do, you will soon experience supernatural strength and discover the victorious life God has planned for you.

ENCOURAGE YOURSELF

"And David was greatly distressed; for the people spake of stoning him, because the soul of all the people was grieved, every man for his sons and for his daughters: but David encouraged himself in the LORD his God."

1 Samuel 30:6

Who encouraged David to carry on in the face of those dire circumstances? We see in this passage that he *"encouraged himself."* David encouraged David. Although it is great to receive encouragement from others when we face adversity, at times we, like David, will have to encourage ourselves. But we note that David did not just *"encourage himself"* but rather *"encouraged himself **in the LORD his God**"* (emphasis added).

Faith is necessary for every mountain to be moved

We all face battles in this life that pose great opportunities to despair as David did, but instead of wallowing in self-pity or giving up, he did the brave thing—he chose to continue for the sake of all who would be adversely affected if he quit! He thought of others not of himself. He also knew that his source of strength was Almighty God.

"The LORD is my strength and my shield; my heart trusted in him, and I am helped: therefore my heart greatly rejoiceth; and with my song will I praise him."

Psalm 28:7

Don't let your situation limit your destination. God doesn't make mistakes. He made you *on purpose*. The struggle you are facing is just evidence of a miracle about to take place in your life. Stand and encourage yourself in the Lord, knowing that angels are working on your behalf to bring you out! An unexpected miracle is coming your way right now! Be encouraged and know that God has a divine purpose for your life.

KEEP YOUR EYES ON JESUS

"And straightway Jesus constrained his disciples to get into a ship, and to go before him unto the other side, while he sent the multitudes away. And when he had sent the multitudes away, he went up into a mountain apart to pray: and when the evening was come, he was there alone. But the ship was now in the midst of the sea, tossed with waves: for the wind was contrary. And in the fourth watch of the night Jesus went unto them, walking on the sea. And when the disciples saw him walking on the sea, they were troubled, saying, It is a spirit; and they cried out for fear. But immediately Jesus spoke unto them, saying, Be of good cheer; it is I; be not afraid. And Peter answered him and said, Lord, if it be thou, bid me come unto thee on the water. And he said, Come. And when Peter was come down out of the ship, he walked on the water, to go to Jesus. But when he saw the wind boisterous, he was afraid; and beginning to sink, he cried, saying, Lord, save me. And immediately Jesus stretched forth his hand, and caught him, and said unto him, O thou of little faith, wherefore didst thou doubt? And when they were come into the ship, the wind ceased. Then they that were in the ship came and worshipped him, saying, Of a truth thou art the Son of God."

Matthew 14:22-33

I want to share with you something very significant in this chapter, something that I hope will help you to keep your eyes fixed on the Master Jesus instead of on the bad situation you may be in right now. Jesus had been preaching and, as usual, had attracted a large crowd. Five thousand men plus women and children had gathered to hear Him, and He not only taught them but also fed them all (possibly as many as 10,000 people) through a miracle of provision. After feeding them, He had sent them away and instructed His disciples to get into a boat and go out onto the Sea of Galilee while He Himself went to be alone to pray.

The Scriptures tell us that while Christ was in prayer the wind became boisterous and the waters of the sea became severely troubled. But in the fourth watch of the night (somewhere between 3 a.m. and 6 a.m.) He went out to the boat, *walking on the water!* When the disciples (who I'm sure were already very concerned about the weather) saw Him they were frightened and thought they were looking at an apparition! Knowing this, Jesus said, *"Be of good cheer; it is I; be not afraid!"*

God doesn't make mistakes

Peter—who for better or worse was always the first to speak up—said, *"Lord, if it be thou, bid me come unto thee on the water!"* So Jesus instructed Peter to come on out to Him. So following Christ's instruction, Peter proceeded to go out to Jesus, and he too was walking on the water until ... he realized what was going on! Seeing that the wind and the waves were tempestuous, Peter was afraid and began to sink down into the water. Peter immediately cried out to the Master, and Jesus stretched out His hand to catch him. And as Jesus caught him, He said, *"O you of little faith, why did you doubt?"* Jesus then took him up and they got into the boat and when they did the storm immediately ceased. In the account of this event in the Gospel of John 6, we read that they were immediately on the other side of the sea. And they all worshipped Jesus, saying, *"Truly, You are the Son of God!"*

How many times during the storms of life do we not sense God's presence only to find in the end that God gives us victory. Unfortunately, many Christians have forgotten that God has promised always to be with us. Hebrews 13:5 says, *"I will never leave thee, nor forsake thee."* This must provide us with immediate comfort, an infusion of courage, and a sense of confidence to endure.

Friend, as long as you hear His Voice and obey His Word, you will be on top of the troubled water. You will weather any storm that you must face on the road to your destiny. Whatever situation troubles you, I declare in Jesus' name that you will be on top of it!

You were made on purpose

The Word of God is an unmovable WORD! It shall not return void, so you can stand on it and expect God's promises to happen any moment! Don't allow desperation to affect your determination! You have come too far to settle for less than the process put you through! Stay focused! When Peter followed the Master's instruction, He was on top of the water, despite how greatly troubled it was. But when he took his eyes off of Jesus and began to look at the troubled, wind-whipped water all around him, he began to sink down into that water. What he was FOCUSED on began to CONSUME him! Those who take their eyes off of God and begin to go their own way sink down into that which they are focused on. This is not your portion in the name of Christ Jesus! AMEN!

When you make praise happen and put your trust in God, you will experience a shift in the atmosphere. You will discover possible opportunities in impossible situations. It does not matter what you are going through or what you have been through. You must understand that GOD has a way of bringing the best you to the surface. Embrace the struggle and let it build up your spiritual muscles.

Let me tell you; IT DID NOT COME TO STAY. IT CAME TO PASS!!!

CHAPTER 4

WEAPONS OF PRAISE

Praise is a powerful weapon of spiritual warfare that has too often been overlooked and neglected. As children of God, we need to utilize all the weapons God has given us as we wage war with the enemy. In Ephesians 6:12, the Bible tells us that our struggles are not with other human beings but with the devil and his demons. Satan, the enemy of our souls, attempts to defeat us with cunning strategy executed through well-laid tactics of deception.

"For we wrestle not against flesh and blood, but against principalities, against powers, against the rulers of the darkness of this world, against spiritual wickedness in high places."

Ephesians 6:12

But the devil is a liar. Jesus called him "the father of lies and of all that is false" (John 8:44 AMP). He tells us things about ourselves, people, and circumstances that are just not true. He does not, however, tell us the entire lie all at once. He begins by bombarding our minds with a cleverly devised pattern of little nagging thoughts, suspicions, doubts, wonderings, reasonings, and theories. He moves slowly and cautiously. He has a strategy for his warfare because he has studied us for a long time. He knows what we like and don't like. He knows our insecurities, weaknesses, and fears. He is willing to invest any amount of time it takes to defeat us. Through careful strategy and cunning deceit, Satan attempts to set up "strongholds" in our minds, which are areas in which we are held in bondage due to a certain engrained way of thinking. But glory be to God for the weapons He has given us to bring into captivity every thought to the obedience of Christ.

THE WORD

"For the weapons of our warfare are not carnal, but mighty through God to the pulling down of strong holds; Casting down imaginations, and every high thing that exalteth itself against the knowledge of God, and bringing into captivity every thought to the obedience of Christ."

2 Corinthians 10:4-5

In this passage the Apostle Paul tells us that we have the weapons we need to overcome Satan's strongholds and that we are engaged in spiritual warfare. Verse 5 shows clearly where the war is waged. The Amplified Bible translation of this verse says that we are to "refute arguments" with these weapons of truth. The devil argues with us, offering theories and reasoning. All this activity goes on in the mind—the true battlefield of spiritual warfare.

One weapon is God's Word received through preaching, teaching, reading, and private Bible study. But we must continue in the Word until it becomes revelation given by inspiration of the Holy Spirit. Jesus said, *"Take heed what ye hear: with what measure ye mete, it shall be measured to you: and unto you that hear shall more be given"* (Mark 4:24). In other words, the measure of thought and study you give to the truth you hear will be the measure of virtue and knowledge that comes back to you. We must continue using the weapon of the Word.

PRAISE AND PRAYER

Praise and prayer are other weapons available to us in waging spiritual warfare. In an earlier chapter we learned that praise defeats the devil faster and more efficiently than any other battle plan. But it must be genuine heart-praise, not just lip service or a method that we are merely "trying" to see if it works. Also, praise and prayer involve the Word. We praise God according to His Word and His goodness.

Prayer is relationship with the Godhead. It is asking for help or talking with God about something that bothers us. To have an effective prayer life, you must develop a good personal relationship with the Father. Know that He loves you, that He is full of mercy, and that He will help you. Get to know Jesus. He is your friend. He died for you. Get to know the Holy Spirit. He is with you all the time as your Helper. Let Him help you.

Embrace the struggle, let it build up your spiritual muscles

Learn to fill your prayers with the Word of God. Even Jesus used the weapon of the Word in the wilderness to defeat Satan (Luke 4:1-13). Each time the devil lied to Jesus, He responded with, *"It is written,"* and then quoted the Word of God to him. The truth is always revealed through the Word. God has ordained your mouth for victory.

"Out of the mouth of babes and sucklings hast thou ordained strength because of thine enemies, that thou mightest still the enemy and the avenger."

Psalm 8:2

Since God has ordained YOUR mouth to stop HIS (your) enemies, what are you waiting for? No wonder the devil works overtime on you! He knows that if he can bombard you with overwhelming situations and circumstances that keep you down and broke, then he can knock your faith level down and get you to doubt both yourself and God. Then he wins because you will never open your mouth and praise God! He makes sure to send disappointments, discouragements, troubles, and tribulations into your life to wear you down and wear you out! My friend, let the devil know: "I MAY BE DOWN, BUT IT AIN'T OVER TILL GOD SAYS IT'S OVER!" HALLELUJAH!!! You need to learn how to look back over your life and review everything the Lord has brought you through. When you do you will surely conclude that what you are going through now is nothing for the Lord to solve!

BE DANCE - FULL!

"Let them praise his name in the dance: let them sing praises unto him with the timbrel and harp."

Psalm 149:3

Although dance has so many wonderful applications and so many beautiful expressions, I must say that it has been particularly exciting for me to discover the power and effectiveness of dance in spiritual warfare.

In 2004, I was invited to minister at IGOC (International Gathering of Champions) in London, Europe's premier Christian conference, hosted by Pastor Matthew Ashimolowo. This was my first time singing in front of 15,000 people—maybe more. Before going on stage, I said to God: "Father, just use me as a point of contact between You and Your people." To keep the story short, after ministering a woman came up to me and said: *"Minister*

Jerry, while you were dancing with all your strength before the throne of glory, the Holy Spirit asked me to dance for my breakthrough! Even though I was in pain for the past two weeks before this gathering, I obeyed the voice of the Lord and then released my faith!" She told me that she had started dancing, running everywhere, shouting, lifting her hands, bowing, making a joyful noise to the Lord. Sudden she realized that the pain was gone! She was doing things that she had not been able to do for weeks.

I have seen the demonstration of God's Spirit and power countless times in the pulling down of strongholds through the weapon of spiritual warfare called dance.

God has ordained your mouth for victory

God has equipped us with many mighty and powerful spiritual weapons designed to successfully pull down these strongholds. Unfortunately, many Christians refuse to accept and use them. Satan knows well that if he can control your thoughts, he can control your actions. If you have any major strongholds in your life that need to be broken, let me encourage you by telling you that God is on your side.

There is a war going on, and your mind is the battlefield. But the good news is that God is fighting on your side!

BENEFITS OF PRAISE
~~~

"Let the people praise thee, O God; let all the people praise thee. O let the nations be glad and sing for joy: for thou shalt judge the people righteously, and govern the nations upon earth. Selah. Let the people praise thee, O God; let all the people praise thee. Then shall the earth yield her increase; and God, even our own God, shall bless us. God shall bless us; and all the ends of the earth shall fear him."

<div align="right">Psalms 67:3-7</div>

Other benefits:

God's Presence is Guaranteed

"But thou art holy, O thou that inhabitest the praises of Israel."

<div align="right">Psalm 22:3</div>

<div align="center">God is enthroned by praise</div>

God's Victory is enforced, His ability is released

"And when they began to sing and to praise, the LORD set ambushments against the children of Ammon, Moab, and mount Seir, which were come against Judah; and they were smitten. For the children of Ammon and Moab stood up

against the inhabitants of mount Seir, utterly to slay and destroy them: and when they had made an end of the inhabitants of Seir, every one helped to destroy another."

2 Chronicles 20:22-23

Praising the Lord releases Mighty Power

IT IS A GOOD THING

"Praise ye the LORD: for it is good to sing praises unto our God; for it is pleasant; and praise is comely."

Psalm 147:1

Nothing is more pleasant to God than praise

IT CAUSES INCREASE AND MULTIPLICATION

"And out of them shall proceed thanksgiving and the voice of them that make merry: and I will multiply them, and they shall not be few; I will also glorify them, and they shall not be small."

Jeremiah 30:1

Divine increase for His people and the Church

PRESERVED BLESSING

"I know that, whatsoever God doeth, it shall be for ever: nothing can be put to it, nor any thing taken from it: and

God doeth it, that men should fear before him."

Ecclesiastes 3:14

It's a covenant

YOU ENTER YOUR INHERITANCE

"Now after the death of Joshua it came to pass, that the children of Israel asked the LORD, saying, Who shall go up for us against the Canaanites first, to fight against them? And the LORD said, Judah shall go up: behold, I have delivered the land into his hand."

Judges 1:1-2

Praise is your surest access into your inheritance

IT KEEPS YOUR FAITH ACTIVE AND STRONG

"He staggered not at the promise of God through unbelief; but was strong in faith, giving glory to God; And being fully persuaded that, what he had promised, he was able also to perform."

Romans 4:20-21

Faith cometh by hearing, and hearing by the word of God

IT CAUSES GOD TO REMOVE SICKNESS FROM YOUR MIDST

"And ye shall serve the LORD your God, and he shall bless thy bread, and thy water; and I will take sickness away from the midst of thee."

Exodus 23:25

Just BELIEVE!!!

IT BRINGS BLESSING, HONOR, PROMOTION, AND INCREASE

"Let the people praise thee, O God; let all the people praise thee. Then shall the earth yield her increase; and God, even our own God, shall bless us."

Psalm 67:5-6

"The righteous shall flourish like the palm tree: he shall grow like a cedar in Lebanon."

Psalm 92:12

You rise and you flourish

"When righteous men do rejoice, there is great glory."

Proverbs 28:12a

 Brothers and sisters, keep praising even when you don't understand what GOD is doing. I am grateful that I know how to praise God through my pain because I understand that praise is the surest access into my inheritance. Don't take your praise for granted. Use it and breakthrough!

Now that you know the power of praise and it benefits, PUSH! **Praise Until Something Happens!**

A drop of praise is an unsuitable acknowledgement for an ocean of mercy!

Don't wait for the storm to be over. Learn how to dance in the rain!

PART II

PRAY UNTIL SOMETHING HAPPENS

CHAPTER 5

POWER OF PRAYER

"Confess your faults one to another, and pray one for another, that ye may be healed. The effectual fervent prayer of a righteous man availeth much. Elias was a man subject to like passions as we are, and he prayed earnestly that it might not rain: and it rained not on the earth by the space of three years and six months. And he prayed again, and the heaven gave rain, and the earth brought forth her fruit."

James 5:16-18

Never underestimate the power of prayer. Elijah, an ordinary man just like you and me, prayed that it would not rain, and the Word of God declares: *"It did not rain on the land for three and a half years. Again he prayed, and the heavens gave rain, and the earth produced its crops."* When prayer goes up, something happens. The power of prayer is the power that comes to you when you realize that God can be your point of reference in the midst of all the confusion of your daily life. That power is the steadfastness of God in contrast to the incomplete, fragile inconstancies of yourself. It is the power that comes when you are able to be centered, anchored in a belief and rooted in a Truth (the Word of God), which is stronger and deeper than the day-to-day truths and lies that you struggle with. It is the constant renewal of perspective.

Prayer

Many think that prayer is just asking God for this and for that, but it is much more than that! Some say that it is a mysterious practice reserved for "super" Christians. I say, "Nonsense!" Prayer is simply communicating with God—listening and talking to Him. It is a fellowship between you "the creature" and GOD "the Creator."

Prayer is the ability to understand and work with the spiritual world. It is your communion with God the Father in which you talk with Him and He talks with you.

Prayer opens your eyes. It extends your horizons. It shines light into the darkness of your fears and your sorrows, your hopes and your joys, your shame and your pride. It gives you new ways of seeing life and relationships, of understanding work and the cost of growing. It is a spiritual channel that connects you with help from above.

The crucial question is thus: "How do we pray?"

How many times have I heard people say, *"I don't know how to pray?"* Some believers have even paid a lot of money to others to pray for them because of their titles: "The Man of God"; "The Prophet of Nations"; etc. Some even go to their pastors with a prayer request and then go home and spend their time sleeping, watching television, shopping—all the while expecting God to answer their request. Dear Friend, don't let the devil fool you! If you want to hear from God then you had better wake up and PRAY! Even though the Bible says we should pray for one another, you are the first person to engage the prayer line to see triumph.

"Let us therefore come boldly unto the throne of grace, that we may obtain mercy, and find grace to help in time of need."

Hebrews 4:16

Notice that the Scripture didn't say *"Let them therefore come"* BUT *"Let US therefore come."* God is just waiting for you to talk to Him, waiting for those few brief moments when you acknowledge Him, think about Him, and show Him your love and reverence. He desperately wants to talk to you, not in words, but through your mind and your heart. In fact, He wants you to invite Him to walk with you in every step you take and every move you make.

Since both your life and future are secure in Him, nothing in your life is ever too dead to hear the voice of God. Pray your way out! And I guarantee you that one word from God will change your entire situation.

LORD, TEACH US TO PRAY

"And it came to pass, that, as he was praying in a certain place, when he ceased, one of his disciples said unto him, Lord, teach us to pray, as John also taught his disciples."

Luke 11:1

Many have been taught that one doesn't need to learn how to pray—that you simply learn to pray by praying. This is a mistaken assumption. Until you are taught or trained, you cannot triumph.

To have an effective and fulfilling prayer life, you need to be taught or trained how to pray. The length of prayer— the quantity of words—does not determine its effectiveness, nor does the eloquence of the words you speak to God. Rather, the quality of the prayer is what determines its effectiveness. What a tragedy when communion with God is reduced to carnal religious egotism. Jesus' disciples knew this, so they asked their Master: *"Teach us to pray, as John also taught his disciples"* (Luke 11:1). And Master Jesus, knowing the importance of training, taught them how to pray.

"And he said unto them, When ye pray, say, Our Father which art in heaven...."

Luke 11:12

First you must have a Father in heaven.

THE LORD'S PRAYER
(The ultimate model of prayer)

"OUR FATHER IN HEAVEN"

Jesus begins by acknowledging God as heavenly Father. This speaks to the intimate relationship between a father and child; it is not a distant relationship. This is the type of relationship that Jesus wants us to have with the Father.

If you are to be welcome on the prayer line, however, you must first have a Father in heaven. Bear in mind that apart from Jesus Christ *no one* can come to the Father. Jesus is the way, and the truth, and the life; no one goes to the Father but through Him (John 14:6).

"HALLOWED BE YOUR NAME"

Almighty God Himself has brought us into His family and given us the privilege of calling Him "Father." Of course, we still need to come with humility, reverence, and awe—and not with the slap-happy attitude of some modern children toward their parents!

Hallowing God's name is more than what you do in prayer and worship. It must be expressed through your daily living. It is one of the keys that gives way to the Father's character and purpose to expressed (revealed) in our lives.

May the Spirit enable you, not just in your praying and praising and worship, but in all of your life to express that petition, *"Hallowed be Your Name"* (the Father's holiness).

"Enter into his gates with thanksgiving, and into his courts with praise: be thankful unto him, and bless his name."

Psalm 100:4

"Your Kingdom come" is a love factor prayer that God cannot shut His ears to

---

"YOUR KINGDOM COME"

The kingdom of God is the most important concept in the Gospel of Matthew. Not only a future hope, the kingdom of God is the rule of God in the universe and is a present reality. When you say: Father let *"Your Kingdom come,"* you are inviting God to come and rule in your life.

You are saying, "Lord, I want to see expansion, your nature, your power, and your glory revealed in my life."

Only the transforming grace of God can change the desires of your heart from *"my kingdom come"* to *"Your kingdom come."* As you continue reading this book, may the grace of our Father in heaven be with you as you seek His KING-DOM in your life, family, work, business, and in every other area of your life. In Christ Jesus' precious name! AMEN!

Wow! What a privilege! To call the Creator and Ruler of the whole universe "Father"!

"YOUR WILL BE DONE ON EARTH AS IT IS IN HEAVEN"

In His prayer to the Father, Jesus teaches a very important lesson. He demonstrates how to subject ourselves to the Father, to accept His will and His way, over our own self-will. In so doing, we bring glory to the Father here on earth as He is also glorified in heaven.

The kingdom of God is the rule of God in the universe and is a present reality

---

"GIVE US TODAY OUR DAILY BREAD"

We should ask our Father each day to provide for our needs, just as He promised He would do in His Holy Word. The Bible says: *"We don't have, because we don't ask."* But this petition in the Lord's Prayer goes beyond that.

Jesus is teaching the disciples to recognize the Father as all-sufficient. He is the provider. Man is not self-sufficient; man is dependent.

Understand that in this part of the prayer you acknowledge that your daily needs are met through the sufficiency of your heavenly Father.

Engage the prayer line to see triumph

"FORGIVE US OUR DEBTS (OR TRANSGRESSIONS) AS WE ALSO HAVE FORGIVEN OUR DEBTORS (TRANSGRESSORS)"

This speaks about forgiveness among our associates, neighbors, friends, family, and loved ones. It is all-inclusive and encompasses every person whom we come in contact with in social or business situations. If you cannot forgive others, how can you expect your heavenly Father to forgive you? In Luke 6:37 Jesus says: *"Forgive, and you will be forgiven."*

"LEAD US NOT INTO TEMPTATION. BUT DELIVER US FROM THE EVIL ONE"

"But the Lord is faithful, who shall stablish you, and keep you from evil."

2 Thessalonians 3:3

The Word says: Our heavenly Father *"will keep us from evil."* We need to ask our Father for protection and to help us recognize every evil thing and every temptation before us.

As a child of God, you have divine protection from temptation and provision for safe passage from the evil one (the enemy, the devil). But to have that access, you will have to ask your Father in heaven.

"The LORD shall preserve thee from all evil: he shall preserve thy soul."

Psalm 121:7

Prayer is simply communicating with God – listening and talking to Him

---

Friend, say this prayer with me:

"Help me, dear Father, to steer clear of that liar and deceiver. Let me see clearly the path that You want me to walk. By the power of the Holy Spirit that dwells within me, may I never stray from Your will and way... In Jesus' name! AMEN!"

LORD'S PRAYER – A GLORIOUS ENDING

Some commentators believe that the end of the Lord's Prayer—**"For thine is the kingdom, and the power, and the glory forever"**—was added by someone other than the original writer. Whether that is true or not, this last phrase simply emphasizes more praise and glory to God the Father, so it is absolutely biblical (and the Holy Spirit saw to it that it became part of God's Word) ... a glorious ending to a model prayer to God!

THE 4 KEYS FOR EFFECTUAL PRAYER:

- Acknowledging God the Father and His will
- Giving gratitude
- Asking for forgiveness
- Beseeching protection and deliverance and giving God praise and glory

---

Acknowledge that your daily needs are met through the sufficiency of your heavenly Father

---

A LIFESTYLE OF PRAYER

Every believer needs to develop a lifestyle of prayer. The Word says, *"Pray without ceasing"* (1 Thessalonians 5:17). You need to realize that you can live in the spirit of prayer, whereby you pray all the time. Your heart can be crying out to God always. Your thought life should never be far away from Him.

One day I asked God: "Father, why is it that some people never feel or sense Your touch in their lives?" And He said, "Son, if my people, which are called by my name, shall humble themselves, and pray, and seek my face, and turn from their wicked ways, then will I hear from heaven, and will forgive their sin, and will heal their land." For God to restore every broken place in our lives, we need to humble ourselves. I believe the reason most Christians don't experience the miraculous touch of God in their lives is that most of their waking moments are consumed with the affairs of this life. Their hearts are far from God.

In Jude 20 the Scripture says, *"But ye, beloved, building up yourselves on your most holy faith, praying in the Holy Ghost."* It is important to pray in the Spirit and keep yourself built up spiritually. Some people are always saying, *"I need to get prayed up."* Don't just get prayed up; stay prayed up. Stay in the Spirit.

The kingdom of God is the rule of God in the universe and is a present reality

---

PRAY IN THE SPIRIT
(Speaking In Other Tongues)

Praying in the Spirit is a wonderful experience that comes from having a relationship with God's Holy Spirit. Jesus told us that God is spirit and His worshipers must worship Him in spirit and in truth (John 4:24). This encouraging word from Jesus helps us make sense of this prayer level.

Without wisdom and guidance from the Holy Spirit, you cannot enter this realm of prayer life. The Bible says that through Christ we all have access to the Father by one Spirit (Ephesians 2:18). To pray in the Spirit is to pray with a sincere, sensible, and affectionate pouring out of your heart and soul to God through Jesus Christ our Lord, with the help of the Holy Spirit who speaks to God in groanings that only He can understand.

"Likewise the Spirit also helpeth our infirmities: for we know not what we should pray for as we ought: but the Spirit itself maketh intercession for us with groanings which cannot be uttered. And he that searcheth the hearts

knoweth what is the mind of the Spirit, because he maketh intercession for the saints according to the will of God."

Romans 8:26-27

Stay in the Spirit

The Apostle Paul had much to say on the subject of speaking in other tongues. He apparently practiced what he preached for he said, *"I thank my God, I speak with tongues more than ye all."* Paul did not say that we do not know how to pray, for we do. We pray to the Father in the name of the Lord Jesus Christ, which is the correct way to pray. But just because we know how to pray does not mean that we know what we ought to pray for. That is why Paul said, *"We know not what we should pray for as we ought: but the Spirit itself maketh intercession for us with groanings which cannot be uttered."*

When you pray in tongues, it is your spirit praying by the Holy Spirit within you. It is the Holy Spirit within you giving you the utterance, and you are speaking it out of your spirit. You do the talking, but the Holy Spirit gives the utterance. By that method the Holy Spirit is helping you to pray according to the will of God, praying for those things that should be prayed for. This is not something that the Holy Ghost does apart from you. He doesn't groan or speak in tongues apart from you. Those groanings come from the Spirit inside you and escape through your lips.

"And they were all filled with the Holy Ghost, and began to speak with other tongues, as the Spirit gave them utterance."

Acts 2:4

In this passage, the Word of God teaches that when we are filled with the Holy Ghost we speak with other tongues as the Spirit of God gives utterance. This is an initial evidence or sign of the Baptism of the Holy Spirit. Therefore, the reason you should speak in tongues is that it is a **SUPERNATURAL EVIDENCE OF THE SPIRIT'S INDWELLING**. The Holy Ghost is not going to do your praying for you. He is sent to dwell in you as a Helper and an Intercessor. He is not responsible for your prayer life; He is sent to help *you* to pray.

Speaking in tongues is praying as the Spirit gives utterance. It is Spirit-directed praying. It eliminates the possibility of selfishness in our prayers.

He gives the utterance

PERSONAL EDIFICATION

"He that speaketh in an unknown tongue edifieth himself; but he that prophesieth edifieth the church."

1 Corinthians 14:4

In other words, anytime you speak in tongues, you are building up your faith and strengthening your spirit. This personal edification is perfectly acceptable and necessary for a healthy Christian life.

Speaking in tongues keeps selfishness out of your prayers. If you pray a prayer out of your own mind and your own thinking, it may be selfish and unscriptural. Too often our prayers are similar to that of the man who always prayed, *"God bless me, my wife, my son, his wife—us four and no more."* With this kind of prayer you cannot prevail!

Why? Because God answers prayers that are according to *His* will. Selfish prayers of the "give-give, me-me, my-my" variety will lead you to defeat.

There is a level of prayer that God always answers.

"Now this is the confidence that we have in Him, that if we ask anything according to His will, He hears us. And if we know that He hears us, whatever we ask, we know that we have the petitions that we have asked of Him."

1 John 5:14-15

DIFFERENT RULES FOR DIFFERENT PRAYERS

Just as there are many different sports each with its own rules, so there are different type of prayer and not all have the same rules. The Bible reveals that there are different types of prayer. Knowing what type of prayer to pray and when to pray it is very important to your prayer life.

There are three prayers among all the others that believers who want to be used of God for His glory need to pray:

- Prayer of Consecration
- Prayer of Faith
- Prayer of Praise and Thanksgiving

PRAYER OF CONSECRATION

When I started writing this page, I asked myself: "How can we be effective in a prayer of consecration if we don't understand the word 'consecration' itself?" So I went turned to the *Oxford Advanced American Dictionary* and found this definition for the word "consecration": *"To give something or someone/yourself to a special purpose."* In the Christian faith, consecration is the voluntary dedication of oneself to God, an offering made deliberately and without any reservation whatever. It is the setting apart to God above all of all that we are, all that we have, and all that we expect to have or be. It is not so much the giving of ourselves to the church or merely engaging in some line of church work. It is a separation of oneself to God, a devotion of all that he is and has to a sacred use.

Your will be done

Jesus prayed this prayer in the Garden of Gethsemane. It was a prayer of consecration: He consecrated His will to do the will of His Father.

"Saying, Father, if thou be willing, remove this cup from me: nevertheless not my will, but thine, be done."

Luke 22:42

Jesus did not want to go to the cross. But He would honor the Father's will as to what He should do. He courageously resolved: *"Yet not my will, but yours be done."* Listen: You cannot have a real relationship with God unless you have a life of consecration and total submission to Him. I have heard many Christians tack *"if it be Thy will"* onto the end of every type of prayer. That isn't what this means at all.

Consecration is about preferring His will above ours—living in obedience to His Word. So we need to know His Word and His direction for our daily lives as the Holy Spirit reveals it. You never pray *if it be Your will* when you know the will of God. This will nullify your prayer. People who say that assume that they are being submissive. Right off they are telling God that they do not have faith in the promises that He made to them. They are saying that they may or may not come true. If it does not come true, then it was not God's will. I can tell you boldly now that such a prayer will not be answered because you are not acting in faith.

Let me give you an example: Take a minister who knows that he is called of God, but he does not know where God wants him to go. He can pray: *"Wherever you want me, I will go. I will go to China or anywhere. Not my will, but Your will be done."* This kind of prayer pleases God, and it is the kind of prayer that all Christians should regularly pray if we want to live a victorious Christian life! "NOT MY WILL, BUT YOUR WILL BE DONE AS IT IS IN HEAVEN"

PRAYER OF FAITH

"If any of you lack wisdom, let him ask of God, that giveth to all men liberally, and upbraideth not; and it shall be given him. But let him ask in faith, nothing wavering. For he that wavereth is like a wave of the sea driven with the wind and tossed. For let not that man think that he shall receive any thing of the Lord. A double minded man is unstable in all his ways."

James 1:5-8

The prayer of faith is rooted in our confidence in God's Word. When you are sure that what you are praying for is God's will for you, you can employ the prayer of faith. The prayer of faith is knowing God's will, praying it, and receiving it from Him.

The two greatest hindrances to prayers of faith are; not forgiving and doubting.

There is a level of prayer that God always answers

PRAYER OF PRAISE AND THANKSGIVING

Praise and worship bring us into the presence of God. Praising God in both the good and bad times affirms our faith in Him. Praise and thanksgiving are powerful weapons. They disarm the two most deadly weapons used against us in our Christian walk: unbelief and satanic attacks. These two things are manifested in many different ways, but praise and thanksgiving is the two-edged sword that helps us fight against evil (see Psalm 100; Acts 16:16-34; Psalm 149:4-9; 1Thessalonians 5:15-19).

Sadly, these three prayers are missing in many believers' lives. Those who desire to have the anointing for their breakthrough would do well to remember that only a consecrated, yielded, praise-full heart will move God.

Prayer is the master strategy that God gives for the defeat and rout of Satan. *"Praying always with all prayer and supplication in the Spirit"* (Ephesians 6:18). Through prayer the Holy Spirit can so empower you that the devil's work is destroyed. The Bible says:

"No weapon that is formed against thee shall prosper; and every tongue that shall rise against thee in judgment thou shalt condemn. This is the heritage of the servants of the LORD, and their righteousness is of me, saith the LORD."

Isaiah 54:17

Jesus says in John 14:13-14:

"And whatsoever ye shall ask in my name, that will I do, that the Father may be glorified in the Son. If ye shall ask any thing in my name, I will do it."

Today, you have amazing privilege and authority in the name of Jesus. Use it! Using His name brings the supernatural dimension into your praying. It clears the way before you. It pushes back the darkness from you. It is the key to heaven's resources. Rejoice in His name! Clothe yourself with His name. Learn to pray with the full authority of the name of Jesus! AMEN!!!

Supernatural

FASTING

Fasting and prayer is one of the most powerful spiritual combinations on earth. True fasting brings humility and alignment with God. It breaks the power of flesh and demons. It kills unbelief and brings answers to prayer when nothing else works. It has been well said that *prayer is not preparation for the battle, prayer IS the battle!* And of all the things we can do to enhance the power and focus of prayer, fasting is doubtless the most potent.

Fasting is where the power is because it puts us in harmony with an All Powerful God who demands humility from those who wish to be close to Him.

Fasting humbles the flesh. When it is done for that purpose, fasting pleases the Spirit of God. You can go a certain distance in your relationship with God, and experience many things, without fasting much, but the highest, richest, and most powerful blessings always come to those who, along with other spiritual disciplines, fast much unto God. The most significant biblical characters (with the possible exception of Abraham) were all men of fasting and prayer. Jesus, the Son of God, was a man of fasting and prayer (Matthew 4:2). So was the apostle Paul (2 Corinthians 11:27). Moses fasted 80 days. Elijah fasted 40 days. The early church fasted before starting any major work. The greatest spiritual leaders of the 20th and 21st centuries who are making an impact are to my knowledge all men of fasting of prayer. To the best of my knowledge, every one of the men who started a significant spiritual movement in Christianity—Luther, Wesley, Finney, Booth—was a man of fasting. In our day, pastors such as Cho, Bonnke, Osborn, Annacondia, Copeland and Jakes are all men of much fasting. If done right, fasting counts a lot with God.

True fasting brings humility and alignment with God

Fasting is not magic, nor does it twist the arm of God. God wants to do many amazing things, and to accomplish them. He looks for those willing to urgently make the corrections needed to come into line with Him. God resists the proud but gives grace to the humble. Successful fasting is also the quickest way to learn patience. It takes patience and endurance to fast for more than a day. Many of God's tests come to us more quickly when we fast, and we have a better opportunity to pass them. We would have to face these tests anyway if we want to go far with God, but without fasting we would face them much later and in a more time consuming and difficult way. We need to "bite the bullet" and embrace the correction God wants to apply to our souls.

Fasting gives you God's focus for your life. It is a major key to hearing God's voice (the other is true worship – and the two are related). We need focus from God more than anything. The world we live in is working overtime to distract us, to entice us, to win our hearts and minds, to command our focus, and to determine our vision.

Fasting cuts out the world so that we can tune into God. If we are obedient to God fasting will make us catalysts for revival and awakening.

Fasting is a major key to hearing God's voice

- **Ezra** the priest fasted for God's protection while carrying valuable things for God's temple. We too can fast for God's protection. (Ezra 8:21-23)

- **Daniel** the prophet fasted for the fulfilment of God's promises and received mighty revelations from God. (Daniel 10:3)

- **Jesus** fasted and spoke the Word of God to overcome Satan (see Matthew 4:1-10; Luke 4:1-13). He fasted to begin His public ministry and to receive the power of God and the anointing. (Luke 4:14)

- **Elijah** needed to fast 40 days before he heard God's voice again. (1 Kings 19:8)

- **Moses** fasted to receive the Ten Commandments and the Law of God and to see God's glory and goodness.

- **The elders, prophets and teachers** in Antioch fasted and ministered to God, which resulted in the launching of Paul and Barnabas' apostolic ministry to the Gentiles (Acts 13:2-3)

Jesus says to us in Matthew 6:16;

"When you fast..." not *"If you fast"*!

Fasting is a wonderful tool God has given us to help bring us to that place. God's ultimate desire is that we live "fasted" lives, thus reducing the need for periodic fasting. Until we come to the place where the kingdom of God means more to us than food, however, we need to set our wills to fast in order to bring our bodies under subjection to the Spirit of the Lord.

Successful fasting is also the quickest way to learn patience

---

Paul was an overcomer. In 1 Corinthians 9:27 he says:

"But I keep under my body, and bring it into subjection: lest that by any means, when I have preached to others, I myself should be a castaway."

For us to overcome we must do likewise. To grow in God we must follow the methods He mapped out in His Word. The Lord is encouraging us to walk in His footsteps so that we might attain the same victory that Paul did. It is not impossible! We just have not understood God's ultimate purpose for our lives. We have lived far below the level God intended. Even though we will walk through some hard places in this life, when we come into the same perfection that Paul did we will be able to say it was worth it all.

"In weariness and painfulness, in watchings often, in hunger and thirst, in fastings often, in cold and nakedness."

2 Corinthians 11:27

God made it clear through the prophet Joel that the outpouring of the Spirit in the last days will be in proportion to our fasting and crying out to God in humility, hunger, and repentance (Joel 1:5; 2:12).

JOIN the fasting warriors today and breakthrough.

CHAPTER 6

THE PLACE OF FAITH

"Now faith is the substance of things hoped for, the evidence of things not seen."

Hebrews 11:1

Faith is belief with strong conviction; firm belief in something for which there may be no tangible proof; complete trust in or devotion to. Faith is the opposite of doubt. It is perhaps the single-most important element of the Christian life. Hebrews 11:6 says: *"But without faith it is impossible to please him: for he that cometh to God must believe that he is, and that he is a rewarder of them that diligently seek him."* This is an incredible statement — yet, it is in the Bible! Take it for exactly what it says. Just think! Anything a person does, in attempting to be Christian, means absolutely nothing if he lacks faith. For without faith, he has no hope and no possibility of pleasing God.

People have often approached me over the years and said: "Minister, I lack faith. I do not feel the presence of God or His power in my life. How can I have more faith?" WHAT ABOUT YOU? Do *you* lack faith to know that God is with you? To overcome sin and guilt? To be healed of disease? To believe all things in His Word? Do you lack faith that "all things [will] work together for good" if you love God (Romans 8:28)? To believe God will work out injustices you have received? To believe God will provide for you? To believe that you can endure severe trials and persecution or that God will deliver you from them? Do you lack faith to see the soon-coming kingdom of God more clearly and believe that you can be in it? Do you have real faith? Is it sufficient for salvation? The Bible says that you need not lack faith in any of these areas! *"For by grace you have been saved through faith. And this is not your own doing; it is the gift of God"* (Ephesians 2:8).

Can you still trust God?

Tell me, have you ever been in a situation that seemed totally barren or hopeless? Have you ever felt like giving up on yourself, your family, or your impossible situation? You might be asking: *"Why all these questions Minister Jerry?"* I want to encourage you and remind you that GOD IS STILL IN THE FAITH BUSINESS.

"Faithful is he who has called you; it is he who shall perform it."

1 Thessalonians 5:24

Faith is not believing that God can but knowing that God will! Let's take a look at the life of Hannah (see 1 Samuel 1:1-28) and discover what she did in the midst of her adverse circumstances. Let's find out what caused this woman of God to receive a mighty breakthrough.

PURSUE GOD FOR YOUR BREAKTHROUGH

Now there was a certain man named Elkanah who had two wives; the name of one was Hannah and the other was Peninnah. Peninnah had children while Hannah had none. This caused much grief and disappointment to Hannah as she desperately wanted to have a male child, but the Lord had closed her womb. Elkanah was very faithful to take his family to the city of Shiloh every year for the purpose of worshipping and offering sacrifices to the Lord of hosts. When it was time for Elkanah to make an offering to the Lord, he would give portions to Peninnah and to all her sons and daughters, but to Hannah he would give a double portion because he loved her.

Peninnah was one who liked to provoke Hannah because of her barrenness. She enjoyed making Hannah's life miserable and as a result of her continuous scoffing, Hannah wept much and refused to eat or drink at the table. Her husband could not understand what she was going through emotionally and once said to her, *"Am I not better to you than ten sons?"* Not realizing what he was saying, he just made matters worse. So Hannah arose from the table and positioned herself before the Lord in prayer. Being in great anguish of soul, she wept bitterly before the Lord until she could weep no more. Her prayers were like sweet incense before the Lord as she set her face like flint in pursuit of Him for her breakthrough miracle.

I believe it's time for you to position yourself before the Lord in prayer for your breakthrough miracle—no matter what. You are on the verge of breakthrough. You can't quit now! You've come too far to turn back. Keep pressing on and pursuing God!

As Eli the priest watched Hannah from the doorpost of the tabernacle, she made a vow to the Lord of hosts. She was a woman determined in her spirit to see a manifestation of her heart's desire come to pass. She was tired of Peninnah's constant chiding and provoking. She was fed up with her barrenness and made a choice to continue in hot pursuit of the Lord and His purpose for her life. Her desire for a man-child caused her to persevere in prayer and faith.

No matter what… You are on the verge of breakthrough

Has the enemy been lying to you and provoking you because of your hopeless situation? Has he told you that you will never come out of this situation victorious? Has he told you that you will never have children because of your barren condition? I urge you today by the Spirit of God to stop listening to the lies of the devil and get on with your life. The Lord of hosts wants to pour out His blessings upon you if you will just learn how to position yourself before Him so that you can receive those blessings.

In 1 Samuel 1:11, Hannah made a vow and said:

"O Lord of hosts, if You will indeed look on the affliction of Your maidservant and remember me, and not forget Your maidservant, but will give Your maidservant a male child, then I will give him to the Lord all the days of his life, and no razor shall come upon his head."

Eli the priest thought Hannah was drunk, but Hannah let him know otherwise. She responded to Eli's false accusation with this: *"I am a woman of sorrowful spirit. I have drunk neither wine nor intoxicating drink, but have poured out my soul before the Lord. Do not consider your maidservant a wicked woman, for out of the abundance of my complaint and grief I have spoken until now."* Wow!

Go in peace!

Have you been falsely accused of wrong doing? Satan's accusers are strategically placed everywhere—in the workplace, school, church, and ministry. You must not allow the false accusations of man to get you down. You must instead learn to set your face like flint to pursue God in the midst of these humiliating accusations and press on toward the victory that God has ordained for you. Eli probably felt like a fool as he kindly responded to Hannah, *"Go in peace, and the God of Israel grant your petition which you have asked of Him."* This was all Hannah needed to break that spirit of oppression and hopelessness over her soul. She received the blessing that Eli spoke over her and went on her way rejoicing in the Lord. FAITH IN ACTION! With a whole new outlook on her situation, she went back to the table and celebrated by eating and drinking her rightful portion. She knew in her spirit that God would bring the needed breakthrough. It was now just a matter of time.

Faith is not believing that God can
but knowing that God will

It is amazing how God can take a hopeless situation and turn it into a time of great rejoicing. One word from God can change your whole outlook on life. Hannah eventually conceived and gave birth to a son whom she called Samuel. She remained faithful in her vow to the Lord and was so grateful for all that the Lord had done for her. She was no longer barren, but fruitful. She was no longer a sorrowful woman, but a woman filled with great joy.

The Lord has a way of silencing our accusers. He has a way of bringing His people through difficult circumstances and situations. That "way" is staying in hot pursuit of Him. When we pursue God with all of our hearts and minds, He will be faithful to grant us the petitions that we have requested of Him.

GOD'S PURPOSES IN OUR DIFFICULTIES

"And we know that all things work together for good to those who love God, to those who are the called according to His purpose. For whom He foreknew, He also predestined to be conformed to the image of His Son, that He might be the firstborn among many brethren."

Romans 8:28-29

If we could choose the number of difficulties we want to face in a month, most of us would pick *zero*: none. Yet God sees value in difficult times. Through His mighty power, He uses trials to accomplish His plans.

One of God's purposes for us is a growing intimacy in our relationship with Him. But He knows that we struggle to put Him first over our own interests. Many of us place higher priority on family and friends than on companionship with God. For others, finances, work, or even personal pleasures interfere. When the Lord sees that our attention is drifting away from Him, He might use hardships to draw us back so that we will refocus.

Another reason God allows difficulties is to conform us to the image of Jesus. You see, pain is a tool that brings areas of ungodliness to the surface. God also uses it to sift, shape, and prune us. The sanctification process, the building of Christ-like character into our lives, starts at salvation and ends with our last breath.

A third purpose for stressful circumstances is to reveal true convictions. Our faith is tested in tough times. It is so easy to say, "God is good," when things are peaceful. But when everything goes wrong, what do we really believe about Him? Do our words and actions reveal an attitude of trust?

King David endured many heartaches: a disintegrating family, personal attacks, and betrayal by close friends. But through his trials, he gained deeper intimacy with God, stronger faith, and more godly character. Won't you let God accomplish His purposes in your present situation?

KEEP THE FAITH

Imagine that you need money to make your car payment. You've tried several options, but they have all failed. Now you are desperate and need God to "work a miracle" on your behalf. What are your options? You could cry, feel sorry for yourself, and say, "I'm a good person. Why doesn't God just help me?" If you take this approach, God will see you crying and sympathize with you, but His Word says, "Without faith it is impossible to please him..." (Hebrews 11:6), so your emotional expression is unlikely to change anything.

To get God to act on your behalf, you could choose to pray a traditional "religious" prayer: *"Lord, You work in mysterious ways. Please stop by my house, God. Please, please, Father! Please don't pass me by...."* This is what I call "the FFP" (Fast Food Prayer) as if God is taking our order at a drive-through window. This is the way many people pray, but this type of prayer does not express faith. It has the form of a prayer, but it lacks the power to produce results. James 1:6 (AMP) says; "that we must ask in faith without wavering or doubting."

The Lord has a way of bringing His people through difficult circumstances and situations
---

As a believer, you have the right to receive answers to every one of your prayers. But the key to getting answers is faith. Whenever you pray or call upon God to help you, you must present evidence of your faith. For example, if you want God to show you how to make your car payment, you have to petition Him correctly:

"Father, your Word says that You will supply all of my needs according to Your riches in heaven. I ask You, Father, to show me how to pay my car note. I surrender this problem to You, and I know that it is already resolved. I thank You, Father, for answering my prayer in Jesus' name."

A faith-filled prayer that is firmly rooted in God's Word will get answers! Faith comes by hearing the Word of God, so build your faith by spending time reading and studying the Word. God's Word (His book of promises) is the evidence you must present to receive the answers you need. His Word is your confession. It is the thing you say to Him in prayer, thereby increasing your faith. Pick up your Bible and find scriptures to match the things you are petitioning God for. Using His Word assures your response. When you know what the Word says about the things you are entitled to receive, you can pray for those things and receive the answers you need. You never have to beg, plead, or bargain with God to have Him answer your prayers. He is moved by your faith in His Word.

His Word is your confession

Show God your faith, and He will show you His love by pouring out His blessings in your life and fulfilling all of the promises He made in His Word.

CHAPTER 7

RELEASE YOUR ANOINTING

It is one thing to be Anointed of God ... and another thing to be in a position to release that anointing.

In this very hour in which we are living, the Lord is releasing His anointing on His people to a degree unseen since the first century. He wants not only to anoint us but to teach us how to steward that anointing, how to release it, and how to increase it in our lives. He wants to give us spiritual victory. It is critically important that we be alert and ready to step into this season of divine appointment. God is calling us to welcome His anointing and take our places in the most glorious hour of the Church.

God is imparting His anointing to us for our own healing and deliverance, but there is more. He wants us to be so empowered and energized with His anointing that we become instruments of His miracles for others. God's anointing breaks the yoke. We are coming into a new prophetic hour, and God is calling us to become carriers of His glory that will break the yokes of bondage, sin, and sickness and set His people free wherever we go.

We are living in a day and age when people are looking for a formula for everything they do in life—including their walk with the Lord. In this chapter I am not attempting to lay out a formula for the anointing. My objective is rather to give you some guidelines concerning the anointing and how to operate in the anointing as a lifestyle.

THE ANOINTING

"The Spirit of the Lord GOD is upon me; because the LORD hath anointed me to preach good tidings unto the meek; he hath sent me to bind up the brokenhearted, to proclaim liberty to the captives, and the opening of the prison to them that are bound; To proclaim the acceptable year of the LORD, and the day of vengeance of our God; to comfort all that mourn; To appoint unto them that mourn in Zion, to give unto them beauty for ashes, the oil of joy for mourning, the garment of praise for the spirit of heaviness; that they might be called trees of righteousness, the planting of the LORD, that he might be glorified."

Isaiah 61:1-3

From above, it is clear that the anointing holds the answer to all the questions of all humanity. When the anointing comes, it binds up the broken-hearted, sets the captives free, opens the prison doors to them that are bound, comforts all that mourn, replacing their sorrow with joy and their ashes with beauty. The anointing clothes us with the garment of praise instead of the oppressive cloak (spirit) of heaviness.

Once this unction comes on a person, all forms of disappointments are converted to supernatural appointments. By this, I mean that everything is compelled to work in his favor: "to appoint unto them." So what is the anointing? It is the empowering of the Spirit of God for supernatural accomplishments. It is the Holy Spirit at work in a man, producing extraordinary results. The anointing is God's device for equipping men to do exploits.

"When she had heard of Jesus, came in the press behind, and touched his garment. For she said, If I may touch but

his clothes, I shall be whole. And straightway the fountain of her blood was dried up; and she felt in her body that she was healed of that plague. And Jesus, immediately knowing in himself that virtue had gone out of him, turned him about in the press, and said, Who touched my clothes?"

Mark 5:30

Jesus Christ always knew the anointing of God and when it was falling around Him. Pressed hard by a great crowd, He sensed immediately that some person was reaching out to Him and had drawn on that anointing. He could sense when it had happened and hence was able to ask pointedly, "Who touched my clothes?" despite the fact that many people were touching Him.

He wants us to be so empowered and energized with His anointing

---

Many times I have been in a meeting and sensed the anointing of God falling like a shower from heaven. As the warmth of the Holy Spirit was falling around me I realised that somebody had reached out to God and that His healing power was touching their body. For example, in 2010, I was invited to the "RENEWAL" worship conference hosted by Noel Robinson (UK). On the first day, the presence of God was so strong during the altar-call that Noel invited me to come down to the front with some other pastors to pray for people. I stood before a girl and the Spirit of God told me to tell her: *"The battle is over; there will be no more pain."* I obeyed the voice of the Lord and boldly repeated what the Holy Spirit said. As I continue praying, the girl whispered in my right ear, "I AM HEALED, Minister, BY HIS GRACE I AM HEALED!"

The anointing is a living and tangible thing that lives in us, takes up residence in us, dwells in us, and, best of all, remains in us. IT NEVER LEAVES US. The reason for this is that we are talking about the Holy Spirit Himself, whom God has promised will come to live in us and never leave nor forsake us.

"And I will pray the Father, and he shall give you another Comforter, that he may abide with you for ever; Even the Spirit of truth; whom the world cannot receive, because it seeth him not, neither knoweth him: but ye know him; for he dwelleth with you, and shall be in you. I will not leave you comfortless: I will come to you."

John 14:16-18

The anointing is God's device for equipping men to do exploits

---

One of the surest ways to diminish the power of the anointing in your life is to neglect your personal relationship with the Holy Spirit and thus to grieve Him. We can grieve Him with our stubbornness, gossip, backbiting other Christians, or through other un-Christ-like words, actions, or attitudes of the heart. Staying in tune with the Holy Spirit requires daily repentance, by which we allow the Holy Spirit to expose our thoughts and attitudes in His perfect light, and turning to Him and His grace to transform us more and more into Christ's image.

Notice three things:

    1. You have an Anointing.

    2. The Anointing abides in you.

    3. The Anointing is there for a purpose.

It is extremely important to understand that it is impossible to understand what the anointing is unless you first know who the Holy Spirit is.

THE HOLY SPIRIT: WHO IS HE?

The Holy Spirit is the third person in the Trinity. He is fully God. He is eternal, omniscient, and omnipresent. He has a will and can speak. He is also the Chief Executive of the divine program on earth. He is the One in charge of the affairs of the kingdom of God on earth today. He is behind every exploit in the Kingdom of God. He is our number one helper in fulfilling our destiny. He is the Spirit of the Lord. If you need wisdom and understanding, counsel and strength, knowledge and fear of the LORD, then He is the right person to connect with! (Isaiah 11:2).

The Holy Spirit has a number of names, titles, and symbols that portray His character and personality. Here are some of the Holy Spirit's titles and attributes:

- **The Power of the Most High** (Luke 1:35)
- **The Breath of Life** (Revelation 11:11)
- **The Helper** (John 14:26)
- **The Comforter** (John 16:7)
- **The Spirit of Access** (Ephesians 2:18)
- **The Spirit of Fruitfulness** (Ephesians 5:9)
- **The "Quickener";** He revives! (Romans 8:11)
- **The Fullness of God** (Ephesians 3:19)
- **The Voice of the Almighty** (Ezekiel 1:24)
- **A Sound from Heaven, as of a Rushing Mighty Wind** (Acts 2:2)

His most popular names are Holy Ghost and Holy Spirit.

THE COMFORTER

In John 16, Jesus described Him "the Comforter."

"Nevertheless I tell you the truth; It is expedient for you that I go away: for if I go not away, the Comforter will not come unto you; but if I depart, I will send him unto you."

John 16:7

God wants to make life comfortable for men. He sent us the Holy Spirit, "The Comforter," primarily to provide comfort to His people. His mission is to make God's people live comfortably. Have you let the Holy Spirit have His way in you completely? Is He not only your Comforter but your friend and your Counselor. He knows every aspect of your past, present, and future. He knows you intimately. He knows your personality, your character, and what you think even before you think it. The Holy Ghost can do more in you, if you let Him, than any counselor here on earth could ever do.

He is our number one helper in fulfilling our destiny

Whatever the situation, God wants to strengthen you and touch your inward parts to help you not only maintain your daily life, but to live above the circumstances you find yourself in. In fact, He wants to make your life comfortable! Paul was in prison when he wrote a good portion of the New Testament. He was more concerned with the church and their condition than his own surroundings. He wanted to encourage them and pray for them. Paul had to find something to help him maintain his daily life while he was in prison. He found it and conveyed that truth in his writings.

"That he would grant you, according to the riches of his glory, to be strengthened with might by his Spirit in the inner man; That Christ may dwell in your hearts by faith; that ye, being rooted and grounded in love, May be able to comprehend with all saints what is the breadth, and length, and depth, and height; And to know the love of Christ, which passeth knowledge, that ye might be filled with all the fulness of God. Now unto him that is able to do exceeding abundantly above all that we ask or think, according to the power that worketh in us, Unto him be glory in the church by Christ Jesus throughout all ages, world without end. Amen."

Ephesians 3:16-21

The Amplified Bible says:

"May He grant you out of the rich treasury of His glory to be strengthened and reinforced with mighty power in the inner man by the [Holy] Spirit [Himself indwelling your innermost being and personality]."

What did Paul mean when he said that the Holy Spirit indwells our innermost being? Or that we should be strengthened and reinforced with mighty power in the inner man by the Holy Spirit"? Paul was saying that for us to encounter the love of Christ that surpasses knowledge and to be filled with all the fullness of God, we have to decrease. We have to die to flesh. We have to come to the point where we realize that we are crucified with Christ and no longer live, but Christ lives in us! (Galatians 2:20)

Brothers and sisters, God wants to strengthen you with His Holy Spirit, to totally indwell with His Spirit your inward parts, your inner being, mind, will, understanding, appetites, emotions, and everything you are.

The Comforter Holy Spirit is your only assured helper from God on earth to help you to maintain your daily life and follow after Christ. He is the One with the strength and power to help you not be tossed and turned with every little breeze that comes your way that is contrary to what you think should happen. When I see what God is doing through the Comforter in my life today, I can testify to you that *God is more than enough for our every need* God can and will do more than we could ever ask, think, guess, imagine, or request in our wildest dreams.

He is the right Person to connect with

WHERE THE SPIRIT IS, THERE IS FREEDOM

"Now the Lord is the Spirit, and where the Spirit of the Lord is, there is freedom."
2 Corinthians 3:17

We are all destined, designed, created to be free. But we forge chains for ourselves and each other, corrupting our freedom till it is no longer freedom at all. Only someone who is not bound by the mess can free us from it. That's where Christ comes in. And, after Christ ascended to the Father, it's where the Holy Spirit comes in. Christ blew on us and sent the Spirit to humanity. The Spirit makes us able to take part in God's work in the world and makes it personal. From there Christ's Gospel becomes *your* Gospel to spread. The Kingdom becomes *your* vision for living. God's hope for all becomes *your* hope for all. God's sorrow over people's situations and deeds becomes *your* sorrow, too. If the Spirit has you, God is not distant but up-close and personal and real.

This new freedom is not something we "have" or possess; it is something that has us just as the Spirit does. The human spirit soars because of the Holy Spirit; otherwise it is still bound to the ground. Change and transformation are inevitable when the anointing of the Holy Ghost comes upon a man. Things that are not working begin to take shape and motion is released. When the anointing comes many other things happen.

You Have an Identity

The anointing gives each person a unique identity among the myriad people in the world.

"But whosoever drinketh of the water that I shall give him shall never thirst; but the water that I shall give him shall be in him a well of water springing up into everlasting life."

John 4:14

You are in Command

God's power makes you a captain. It puts you in charge of the affairs around you. It charges you to be in charge, on top of situations and circumstances.

"Then Samuel took a vial of oil, and poured it upon his head, and kissed him, and said, Is it not because the LORD hath anointed thee to be captain over his inheritance?"

1 Samuel 10:1

It Brings Discovery

When the anointing comes, whatever has been hidden or lost is found. The anointing Spirit opens the eyes to see good and great things. Secrets are revealed and new discoveries are made.

"When thou art departed from me to day, then thou shalt find two men by Rachel's sepulchre in the border of Benjamin at Zelzah; and they will say unto thee, The asses which thou wentest to seek are found: and, lo, thy father hath left the care of the asses, and sorroweth for you, saying, What shall I do for my son?"

1 Samuel 10:2

He is the Comforter

IT COMPELS PROGRESS

It takes the anointing of the Holy Spirit to terminate stagnation and compel progress. Isaiah 10:22 says: *"For though thy people Israel be as the sand of the sea, yet a remnant of them shall return: the consumption decreed shall overflow with righteousness."* The yoke of delay is destroyed and enchantment spreads.

"Then shalt thou go on forward from thence, and thou shalt come to the plain of Tabor, and there shall meet thee three men going up to God to Bethel, one carrying three kids, and another carrying three loaves of bread, and another carrying a bottle of wine."

1 Samuel 10:3

IT ATTRACTS FAVOR

The anointing creates a aura of favor around you that makes men notice you and bless you. Your life smells with the sweet fragrance of beauty and favor (Psalm 45:8-12).

"And they will salute thee, and give thee two loaves of bread; which thou shalt receive of their hands."

1 Samuel 10:4

IT TURNS YOU TO A SIGN

Signs and wonders follow you when the anointing comes on you. Situations and circumstances bow to you and you command proofs at will.

"But the LORD said unto Samuel, Look not on his countenance, or on the height of his stature; because I have refused him: for the LORD seeth not as man seeth; for man looketh on the outward appearance, but the LORD looketh on the heart."

1 Samuel 16:7

It takes the anointing of the Holy Spirit to terminate stagnation and compel progress

---

YOU ARE DIVINELY PROTECTED

The anointing ensures the security of the anointed. *"Touch not mine anointed, and do my prophets no harm"* (Psalm 105:15). The power of God on your life renders your enemies humiliated!

"I have found David my servant; with my holy oil have I anointed him: With whom my hand shall be established: mine arm also shall strengthen him. The enemy shall not exact upon him; nor the son of wickedness afflict him. And I will beat down his foes before his face, and plague them that hate him."

Psalm 89:20-23

YOU ARE DESTINED FOR GREATNESS

"For I know the thoughts that I think toward you, saith the LORD, thoughts of peace, and not of evil, to give you an expected end."

Jeremiah 29:11

In other words, you were set apart for a special purpose in life and called to use that life to bless others. That's what God has destined you for—*greatness!* God anoints us so that He can administer the Kingdom in us and through us. This anointing is God's ability to fulfill the purpose that He has ordained and called each one of us into. Everyone—and especially every believer—has a purpose. God does not create or call people into wantonness (shameless). No! On the contrary, He has a plan and purpose for everyone. Oh, yes!

I know that people will try to put you in a box. They have labeled you: poor, broken home, old, fat, no child, no degree, divorced, single, depressed, kids on drugs, husband alcoholic, disgraced family background, and so on. Friend, you have to learn how to fight all these stereotypes that would lock you in a box. You must get out of that box because you are destined for greatness! You do not realize just how close you are to the success or greatness God has destined for you today. There is a dream in you that is bigger than what you see; it is the real you who is the destined for the greatness God has deposited. If you don't see the potential or seed in yourself, God has ordained someone to recognize the seed of greatness in you.

Maybe you have not yet discovered your purpose or calling in life. That does not mean, however, that God does not have a purpose for you. All you need to do is ask the giver of the anointing "Holy Spirit" to help you discover the purpose that God has for your life. If you know what God has called you to do, then this is the right time for you to tap the power of the Holy Spirit in you! Through the anointing, the Lord has filled you with His power. He wants you to walk into it so that He can pour out His love, His blessings, His compassion, and His healing mercy over the world. In His grace and might God has given you the anointing to achieve the purpose and calling that He has ordained for you. This anointing is by the grace of God. It is not something that we can earn or buy. It is totally a gift of God!

There is a dream in you that is bigger than what you see

In Matthew 28:18-19, Jesus said to His disciples (that is, to *us*): "*All power is given unto me in heaven and in earth. Go ye therefore, and teach all nations, baptizing them in the name of the Father, and of the Son, and of the Holy Ghost.*" Now tell me, how can you impact your environment, your family, friends, colleagues, classmates, and others if you keep this authority or power locked up inside you? God didn't give us this ANOINTING to keep it! He gave it so that we would let it flow through our lives to IMPACT our generation for His Kingdom.

God wants EVERY Christian to do greater things than Jesus did on earth (see John 14:12). You don't need to have experience to be used by God. You don't need to have a degree or a special push from a special pastor or someone else. You just need to be available to the Holy Spirit. Jesus is in the business of using "nobody's." God is drawn to your *in-capability*. He has the power to create everything out of nothing. The Apostle Paul said that the whole creation is awaiting, hoping for, and expecting the manifestation of the sons of God (Romans 8:19). The question then is: *Who are the "sons of God" that Paul is talking about?*

The Scriptures make it clear that through the resurrection of Jesus Christ from the dead we have been born again (1 Peter 1:3-9). John said: *"Behold, what manner of love the Father hath bestowed upon us, that we should be called the sons of God"* (1 John 3:1). So the answer is: *We* are the sons of God, and the world is waiting for our manifestation!

When the anointing comes on you signs and wonders will follow you

---

I don't care who you are, how much education you have, how knowledgeable of the Bible you are, how shy you are, or how unprepared you feel. God can and will use you to further His kingdom. God isn't looking for super-spiritual Christians or those who seem to have it all together. He wants to use you! This is your time! You are in your season! Let God use you today to bless someone! I know that this may be hard to comprehend, especially when it seems as though everything around you is saying the exact opposite. But the truth is that God wants you to step out and take this generation for His Kingdom. He wants to use you now, wherever you are. He said *GO and make disciples of all nations!*

JUST DO IT!

You have to do something with the authority that God has given you. God didn't give you the anointing just so you could sit on the bench and be a cheerleader. God wants every one of us in the game. If you are reading this book, I can guarantee that this is true for you, because if God didn't have something for you to do, you would already be in heaven. Maybe you are shaking your head and thinking: "Jerry, you have absolutely no clue. God cannot use me because of my lack of abilities, or family circumstances, or my shyness, or whatever [fill in the blank]."

If that sounds like you, then God sent me to tell you what He told Joshua: *"Be strong and of a good courage; be not afraid, neither be thou dismayed: for the LORD thy God is with thee whithersoever thou goest."* Remember, the world is waiting for your manifestation. It is time for you to join this great move of God in these end times. God is indeed counting on you to change this earth. So step out and release your anointing! Set your mind on impacting your generation. No matter what area you are in—business, education, entertainment, etc.—God wants to step in and establish His Kingdom through you and your Holy Spirit anointing! If you set your mind and heart on becoming a blessing, then God will remove any blindness and allow you to see opportunities for advancing His kingdom! Make up your mind today to become a kingdom promoter.

To release the anointing simply means you have to do something with the authority that God has given you

God tells each and every one of us the same thing He told the Apostle Paul: *"My grace is sufficient for thee: for my strength is made perfect in weakness"* (2 Corinthians 12:9). You see, God could use those who feel confident in their abilities, but many times He doesn't so that His power can be seen and then there is no way we can let pride step in because we weren't really the ones doing the job—He was.

So no matter where you are today, let me encourage you to not be afraid to let God use you through the SUPERNATURAL POWER OF HIS HOLY SPIRIT. There is nothing that serves as a better faith builder than allowing God to move through you, for that is the only way the world will come to know Him.

CHAPTER 8

YOUR PATH TO VICTORY

Do you need God to make a way out of no way? The swiftness and surety of your deliverance starts with how you respond to hard times and difficult situations. Hear me when I say that it is not just enough to thank God and honor Him only when you have received a blessing. God wants you to show the extent of your faithfulness and trust in Him even in the midst of a challenge. The power of your praise will determine the magnitude of your breakthrough.

As we all know, praise is not just clapping your hands or applauding God. Praise is showing respect, honor, and gratefulness using your whole heart, mind, spirit, and body despite your circumstances. Paul and Silas didn't wait until they experienced a breakthrough to praise and thank God. In the midst of difficult circumstances, they praised God and received the breakthrough they desired.

Acts 16:25-26 reveals:

"But at midnight Paul and Silas were praying and singing hymns to God, and the prisoners were listening to them. Suddenly there was a great earthquake, so that the foundations of the prison were shaken; and immediately all the doors were opened and everyone's chains were loosed!"

Paul and Silas praised God even when their backs were bleeding and their feet and hands were in chains. They praised God despite the pain and suffering they were going through; and, as a result, God shook the very foundations of the prison, setting them free. God will shake the foundation of your prison; your bondage, your problem...if you make a decision to praise and give Him thanks, *no matter what.*

Praising God should become second-nature for all believers. *"This will be written for the generation to come, That a people yet to be created may praise the LORD"* (Psalm 102:18). We were created to praise God, and praise will become a natural expression of our love for the Father when we spend time in the Word and meditate on His goodness.

When you have a heart for God and know that He loves you, your confidence in His ability to deliver you soars. You know help is on the way and you eagerly anticipate it. 1 Thessalonians 5:16-18 (NLT) encourages: *"Always be joyful. Never stop praying. Be thankful in all circumstances, for this is God's will for you who belong to Christ Jesus."* God doesn't tell us to thank Him for negative circumstances; He says to thank Him while we are in the midst of them. Doing this shows that we trust Him to bring us out.

The storms of life will surely come; but don't let them disturb your peace and affect your thoughts and emotions. This will only move you into self-pity and frustration. Instead, maintain an attitude of praise. Your first line of defense is the Word of God. Meditate on it and give it life by speaking it over your circumstances. If you need healing meditate on Scriptures that reveal God's ability to heal. Receive that Word in your spirit and begin praising God for your healing.

The Word of God declares:

"Rejoice in the Lord always. Again I will say, rejoice! Let your gentleness be known to all men. The Lord is at hand. Be anxious for nothing, but in everything by prayer and supplication, with thanksgiving, let your requests be made

known to God; and the peace of God, which surpasses all understanding, will guard your hearts and minds through Christ Jesus."

Philippians 4:4-7

When you are in a situation and there seems to be no way out, open your mouth and praise the Lord—praise, and don't stop. Instead of crying and complaining, give God praise because you know that He has a plan for you that includes deliverance, restoration, and peace. Thank Him for His goodness because your praise will stop the enemy and move the hand of God. When your deliverance comes, continue to praise Him because He has more in store for you. Thank Him for that breakthrough in your home, on your job, and with your children. Through your authority in Jesus, place a demand on your breakthrough and watch God show up in your life in ways you would have never imagined.

Rejoice in the Lord always. Again I will say, rejoice!

DON'T WORRY! BE HAPPY!

"Rejoice evermore. Pray without ceasing. In every thing give thanks: for this is the will of God in Christ Jesus concerning you."

1 Thessalonians 5:16-18

In every difficult situation, such as the temptation in Matthew 4, Jesus concentrated on the truth of Scripture and the character of His Father. We must do likewise. Because we know that if we focus on the problems, we can make ourselves as miserable as we choose to be.

Romans 8:28 says:

"And we know that all things work together for good to those who love God, to those who are the called according to His purpose."

God says that *"all things work together for good to those who love Him...."* And I believe you are a lover of God! You are one of those who are called according to His purpose. As you are going through a midnight experience, remember that midnight is actually the start of a New Day. Sometimes God uses pain or what you call a "problem" to get the job done. The Psalmist says that we should *"come before His presence with singing... Enter into His gates with thanksgiving, And into His courts with praise"* (Psalms 100:1-5). Please note that God's presence has a gate. You can enter freely with thanksgiving and enter His courts with praise.

Of course, you DON'T have to enter by the gate. It's optional; it's always a choice. You can stand stubbornly outside the walls, hoping to get God's attention by the volume of your complaining (worrying attitude). That's *Ordinary Life*. BUT friend, you don't have to settle for *Ordinary Life*. You can be transformed by praising God with a joyful attitude, especially in times of trouble when you are really hurting.

"For I know the thoughts that I think toward you, saith the LORD, thoughts of peace, and not of evil, to give you an expected end."

Jeremiah 29:11

The problems you face will either defeat you or develop you, depending on how you respond to them. God says He has plans for you, "plans to prosper you and not to harm you, plans to give you hope and a future." Unfortunately most people fail to see how God wants to use problems or difficult situations for good in their lives. They react foolishly and resent their problems rather than pause to consider what benefit they might bring. God is at work in your life even when you do not recognize it. But it's much easier and more profitable when you cooperate with Him. Let's take a look at how all things work together for our good even in the storm.

Begin praising God for your healing

---

* "Problems" here means "difficult situations or circumstances."

GOD USES "PROBLEMS" TO DIRECT YOU

Sometimes God must light a fire under you to get you moving. Problems often point us in a new direction and motivate us to change. Is God trying to get your attention? *"Sometimes it takes a painful situation to make us change our ways.* (Proverbs 20:30, GN)

GOD USES "PROBLEMS" TO INSPECT YOU

People are like tea bags...if you want to know what's inside them, just drop them into hot water! Has God ever tested your faith with a problem? What do problems reveal about you? *"When you have many kinds of problems, you should be full of joy, because you know that these problems test your faith, and this will give you patience."* (James 1:2-3, NCV)

GOD USES "PROBLEMS" TO CORRECT YOU

Some lessons we learn only through pain and failure. It's likely that as a child your parents told you not to touch a hot stove. But you probably learned by being burned. Sometimes we only learn the value of something...health, money, a relationship, by losing it. *"...it was the best thing that could have happened to me, for it taught me to pay attention to your laws."* (Psalm 119:71-72, LB)

Sometimes God uses pain or what you call a "problem" to get the job done

---

GOD USES "PROBLEMS" TO PROTECT YOU

A problem can be a blessing in disguise if it prevents you from being harmed by something more serious. Last year a "friend" was fired for refusing to do something unethical that his boss had asked him to do. His unemployment was a problem, but it saved him from being convicted and sent to prison a year later when management's actions were eventually discovered. *"You intended to harm me, but God intended it for good..."* (Genesis 50:20, NIV)

GOD USES "PROBLEMS" TO PERFECT YOU

Problems, when responded to correctly, are character builders. God is far more interested in your character than your comfort. Your relationship to God and your character are the two things you will take with you into eternity. *"We can rejoice when we run into problems...they help us learn to be patient. And patience develops strength of character in us and helps us trust God more each time we use it until finally our hope and faith are strong and steady."* (Romans 5:3-4, LB)

Plans to prosper you and not to harm you, plans to give you hope and a future

---

Today, I would like to encourage you like Paul and Timotheus: *"Keep on rejoicing in the Lord at all times..."* (Philippians 4:4). No matter what storm clouds may rock this ship of yours, the light of Our Savior Jesus Christ will lead you safely through the night. Great glory shall be revealed through your life as you stand on God's promises and hold on to your testimony! As you go through your storms, trust God. Your victory and His glory are on the way!

"For I reckon that the sufferings of this present time are not worthy to be compared with the glory which shall be revealed in us."

Romans 8:18

Fear not. You have survived storms bigger than this one. You are coming OUT! So don't worry! Just BE HAPPY!!!

PART III

PERSIST UNTIL SOMETHING HAPPENS

CHAPTER 9

POWER TO PERSIST AND PERSEVERE

"Behold I am doing a new thing. Can you not perceive it?"

Isaiah 43:19

Do you have a vision of victory for your life? Do you perceive victory in your every step? Are you living each day filled with faith and expectancy? The verse above does not say that God is going to do a new thing *some* day. He didn't say maybe next week, next month, or next year. God said, *"I am doing something new in your life right now!"* Can you not perceive it? God wants to do something new in your life today. Let go of your old way of thinking and take hold of the new thing God has for you!

You may be going through hell right now. The fact of the matter is that you must accept the reality that God the Father, creator of heaven and earth, is trying to mold you and transform you. God wants to change you into what He has declared as His purpose for your life, and that which He spoke about in His written Word. The adverse situation you are in is an opportunity to allow God's Word to come alive in your life and see you through to victory. You can't run from everything that is hard in your life and expect God to deliver you immediately. God uses these challenges to stretch you and enlarge your vision.

The Living Word says: You are more than a conqueror through Jesus Christ who loves you (Romans 8:37). You are the righteousness of God in Christ Jesus (Romans 3:22).

Greater is He who is in you than he who is in the world (1 John 4:4). You have the power to tread upon serpents and scorpions and over all the power of the enemy (Luke 10:19). No weapon formed against you shall prosper (Isaiah 54:17). You really are the head and not the tail, above and not beneath, the rich and not the poor (Deuteronomy 28:1213). You are indeed what God's Word says you are. Remain faithful during your time of adversity. Make up your mind to serve God and persist *no matter what comes against you,* and God will honor you.

We are in a battle against the forces of darkness that specialize in perpetrating wickedness.

That is why God said in Isaiah 43:2:

"When thou passest through the waters, I will be with thee; and through the rivers, they shall not overflow thee: when thou walkest through the fire, thou shalt not be burned; neither shall the flame kindle upon thee."

The adverse situation you are in is an opportunity to allow God's Word to come alive in your life and see you through to victory

---

God says He will be with US *when* not *if* we pass through water and fire. If God gave you a vision for something, you have to know that the devil will not sit idly by. You have to fight the devil for the vision, tooth and toenail, every single step of the way. Any time you take a step forward, the enemy will try to bring opposition and adversity against you. Stand and fight! It is God's desire that we grow and reach our full potential. God is always giving us opportunities to move forward in life. As Paul said: *"For a great door and effectual is opened unto me, and there are many adversaries"* (1 Corinthians 16:9). God promises that through Him we can overcome any opposition the enemy brings our way. He says He will be with us!

We are in a battle against forces of darkness that specialize in perpetrating wickedness

---

YOU ARE APPROVED

"Before I formed thee in the belly I knew thee; and before thou camest forth out of the womb I sanctified thee, and I ordained thee a prophet unto the nations."

Jeremiah 1:5

You are approved by Almighty God! Isn't that awesome? You are created in His image, and you are the apple of His eye. You did not choose God, but He chose you and He is pleased with you—His most precious creation.

Notice that verse does not say that God approves you as long as you don't have any faults or as long as you don't make any mistakes. No, God approves you unconditionally. No matter how many weaknesses you may think you have today, no matter how many times you fall, you have to get right back up again and hold your head up high. Don't allow the enemy to bring strife into your life by deceiving you into thinking that you are not "good enough." Stand strong in your thoughts about yourself, knowing that not only have you been chosen, but you are approved by Almighty God!

HOLD ON! HELP IS ON THE WAY

One of the most powerful, poignant, and punitive words in the English language is the word "Help!" For it is a word that admits a position of total desperation and humility.

Dr. James Merritt well described the meaning of the word help when he said **HELP:** "is the cry of a man sitting at a table surrounded by a stack of unpaid bills, hungry children, and an empty bank account with no job in sight. **HELP:** is the cry of a woman who for years has poured her life into a marriage only to have her husband say, "I'm leaving. I've found someone else, and I don't love you anymore." I don't know about you, but I've found myself many times in a position that I needed help. More than that, I've been in the place where the only One who could possibly help me was the Lord.

"I will lift up mine eyes unto the hills, from whence cometh my help. My help cometh from the LORD, which made heaven and earth. He will not suffer thy foot to be moved: he that keepeth thee will not slumber. Behold, he that keepeth Israel shall neither slumber nor sleep. The LORD is thy keeper: the LORD is thy shade upon thy right hand. The sun shall not smite thee by day, nor the moon by night. The LORD shall preserve thee from all evil: he shall preserve thy soul. The LORD shall preserve thy going out and thy coming in from this time forth, and even for evermore."

Psalm 121

In this psalm we see the Psalmist in dire need of help. He has landed in a place, no doubt, where he has exhausted all other means, measures, and methods of trying to find help. Yet still he has found none. It seems, however, that as he begins to remember and reflect upon some things he suddenly realizes that although it may look dark, dismal, and disappointing, thank God, "Help is on the way!"

The LORD shall preserve thy going out and thy coming in from this time forth, and even for evermore

---

Circumstances beyond our control will *sometimes* prevent us from landing. Disobedience will *always* prevent us from landing and will keep us going round and round. Whatever your circumstances may be, know that there is nothing too hard for God! Jesus is everywhere, all of the time, and like the air traffic controller in the tower, He wants you to have a safe landing! He knows when we need to move and when we need to stand still.

No matter where you are in life right now, God has much more in store for you. God wants to take you to new levels in every area of your life. He wants to give you more wisdom so you can make better decisions. He wants to give you a stronger anointing so you can have greater influence. He wants to bless you financially so you can be a blessing to others. Don't get stuck in the same old rut! There is so much more to life! God has new frontiers for you to explore and higher mountains for you to climb! I can tell you with great confidence that your best days are right out in front of you!

Remember: God will not waste anything you go through in life. You are growing. You are maturing. You are being prepared for promotion. Simply remain faithful and fight through life's trials and tribulations. In due season, in God's appointed time, He will promote you to new levels of victory, and you will live that abundant life that He has promised you! Now, begin to think the way

God thinks. The Bible says, "The path of the righteous grows brighter and brighter and brighter." Think increase.... Think big.... Think expansive! Start expecting the unexpected and look at life through your eyes of faith.

When you do, God will show up and begin to work things out in your favor. The next time you are in a traffic jam (difficult situation or circumstances), instead of complaining and murmuring, think about how the Lord is protecting you from the danger up the road.

There is nothing too hard for God

Let me remind you, my friend that great growth does not come into your life through mountaintop experiences. It comes through the valleys and low places where you feel limited and vulnerable. The prerequisite for the mountain is the valley. If there is no valley, there is no mountain. The time God is really moving in your life may seem to be the lowest moment you have ever experienced. But don't worry! God often allows things to get worse right before He makes them better!

The blessing is the reward that comes after you learn obedience through the things you suffered while waiting for it! Today, take a step towards victory in your life and hold on! Don't panic, pray! Don't worry, worship. Don't tremble, trust! HELP is on the way!!!

CHAPTER 10

HAVING DONE ALL, STAND!

Christians need to realize that everything we face in life is going to demand a response. How we respond is very important. Every one of us will experience some type of crisis. And, if we are not careful, it will shake our very foundation and cause us to go under. Take a skyscraper and destroy its foundation and see what happens to it. It will not stand. You cannot destroy the foundation of something and expect it to remain standing.

You may have a vision or a dream for your personal ministry, your business, or your life. You envision something the way you believe God would have it, but then you come under attack. It seems as though all of your dreams and plans are threatened. It looks like it isn't going to work, and that demands a response. Whether you know it or not, how you respond when a crisis comes will determine how well you will be able to STAND. You may be thinking, "Oh, I've done everything I can to stand—praying, praising, fasting, etc." No, you haven't! If you had, then you would still be standing. You can't tell me you've done all you can to stand while you're buckled over and falling to the ground.

In Mark 11:22 Jesus tells us what to do when a crisis comes: *"HAVE FAITH IN GOD."* When you are in the valley of sorrow, the tears in your eyes can obscure the vision of who is on the mountain-top. Jesus was there on the day of creation. Jesus walked in the midst of a fiery furnace with three faithful men who refused to bow to an idol Jesus shut the jaws of lions to protect Daniel through the night. Jesus walked on this earth and reminded men that He was (and is) the "Great I Am" spoken of in the Old Testament. Jesus proclaimed loudly and clearly, "I am the light of the world" (John 8:12); "I am from above" (John 8:23); "before Abraham was, I am" (John 8:58); "I am the door" (John 10:7); "I am the good shepherd" (John 10:14); "I am the son of God" (John 10:36); and "I am the resurrection" (John 11:25). This same Jesus comes from before the history of this world to stand beside you in the midst of whatever you are going through.

The storms of life will surely come

"Wherefore take unto you the whole armour of God, that ye may be able to withstand in the evil day, and having done all, to stand. Stand therefore, having your loins girt about with truth, and having on the breastplate of righteousness; And your feet shod with the preparation of the gospel of peace; Above all, taking the shield of faith, wherewith ye shall be able to quench all the fiery darts of the wicked. And take the helmet of salvation, and the sword of the Spirit, which is the word of God."

Ephesians 6:13-17

Every battle is a fight for territory. The territory we fight for as soldiers of our God is mostly spiritual and realms of authority. Sometimes a certain place on earth or a place of authority has much influence in the spiritual realm. There are gates of authority—certain places where words spoken there affect many people. Dr. Lance Wallnau (teacher and speaker) identified seven realms of influence on earth: business, government, family, religion, media, education, and entertainment. And I believe that God wants to have us influence and authority in every one of these realms here on the earth, so that the gospel might be preached in all of the earth.

There is only so much that we as humans can do. Oftentimes part of the anxiety comes from wanting to do more than we are able. We blame ourselves, and even though we know better we allow Satan to beat on us as well. This is why we are told in Ephesians 6:13-17 to put on the entire armor that God has given to us. In verse 13, we read *"...that you may be able to withstand in the evil day, and having done all to stand."* The purpose of armor is to protect. The Bible tells us that we are to protect the lower portion of the body with TRUTH. What is the truth? The truth is that Jesus is in control—not Satan, not emotions, not even you! But JESUS, the great I AM! He is the way, the truth, and the life (John 14:6).

Every battle is a fight for territory

The way through the situation is to put God first. By focusing our hearts on God and magnifying His name and praising Him, we fight with certain victory. We see this clearly in the Israelites' crossing over the Jordan River.

"And Joshua said unto the children of Israel, Come hither, and hear the words of the LORD your God. And Joshua said, Hereby ye shall know that the living God is among you, and that he will without fail drive out from before you the Canaanites, and the Hittites, and the Hivites, and the Perizzites, and the Girgashites, and the Amorites, and the Jebusites. Behold, the ark of the covenant of the LORD of all the earth passeth over before you into Jordan."

Joshua 3:9-11

Putting the ark of the covenant first meant trusting God for all that would follow crossing into the new territory. There would be giants to slay, but God was the commander in chief, the Captain of the Lord's Host. You see, the battle you are facing is most likely a battle for territory. Even though your victory is certain, as long as you continue you will face opposition. The devil would like you to quit or to turn back or to be distracted. You must not be distracted. KEEP YOUR FOCUS AND PUSH!!! It is time to be aggressive and energetic when it comes to letting go of the past and pressing forward to the abundant life God has in store for you. It is time to rise up and boldly go after your victory! It is time to develop a warrior mentality and proactively pursue the happiness, health, and peace that God has promised in His Word. Paul said:

"Brothers and sisters, I know that I have not yet reached that goal, but there is one thing I always do. Forgetting the past and straining toward what is ahead, I keep trying to reach the goal and get the prize for which God called me through Christ to the life above."

Philippians 3:13-14

God told Joshua to cross over the Jordan and go into possess the land. "Possess" implies action. It means to drive out the previous tenants. Jesus said in Matthew 11:12, *"The kingdom of Heaven suffers violence, but the violent take it by force."* Friend, the Word of God is your weapon. You are clothed in the armor of God. You must be consistent. You must be persistent. You are not of those who turn back. There is nothing for you in the past. You press forward. It is time to stop dwelling on past mistakes and failures and determine to never look back! Say *Bye-Bye!* to yesterday and PUSH!

As you set your focus on the Word of God, on His promises and giving Him your best praise, you will discover His abundance of joy, peace, and prosperity in every area of your life!

BONUS MATERIAL

HISTORY MAKERS

HISTORY MAKERS

~~~

THE PERSISTENCE OF GOD THAT CHANGES THE WORLD!

As J. Harrison said; "Throughout the Holy Bible we recognize the drive of God in the persistence of men and women who made a difference for the good of the people even against all odds. It did not matter what they faced or whether they stood all alone because they knew that the drive and direction God gave them would strengthen their faith to serve the people.

- **NOAH** did not quit his task when the people mocked him for building a boat when they had never experienced rain.

- **ABRAHAM** did not disobey God when the Lord gave him instructions to take Isaac to the altar of sacrifice, nor did he give up on pleading with God to spare the righteous in the land of Sodom and Gomorrah before it was destroyed.

- **JOSEPH** did not give up just because others gave up on him and betrayed him or because of his circumstances in life.

- **MOSES** never asked for his job nor did he even think

that he was qualified.

- **RUTH** remained strong in character and true to God even when the society around her was collapsing.

- **SAMUEL** did not go back to sleep when Eli told him to just lie back down!

- **DAVID** was the least of all his brothers but had the heart of a lion when someone spoke against our living God.

- **ESTHER** risked her life for the life of others when she went against the traditions the people followed.

- **JOB** did not give in to Satan when he suffered so greatly even when those around him made false accusations.

- **DANIEL** never gave in to man for what he knew was right in his heart by God!

- **NEHEMIAH** did not give in just because the task was so large and the people that he had to face were so opposed to him!

- **JOHN THE BAPTIST** did not detour from God's calling because the way people looked at him for how he appeared on the outside because he knew who was directing him on the inside!

- **JESUS CHRIST OUR LORD AND SAVIOR** did not detour from God's message when He taught us how to love and forgive those who do not understand God's eternal plan in this fallen world.

- **THE FOUR MEN WHO BELIEVED IN THE LORD** did

The Persistence of God that Changes the World!

not let their friend fade away just because they had to carry him and lower him through the roof to be healed!

Nor did

- **PAUL** allow his previous life to detour him from the message that he was to deliver when he saw the light in Jesus Christ!

- **MARTIN LUTHER** did not give in to the Pope nor to the Roman Catholics when he took a stand in 1517 strongly opposing perverted teachings of the church and following God.

- **BENJAMIN FRANKLIN** did not allow his age to stop him, so at 70 years old he helped his country win the American Revolution.

- **JAMES ARMISTEAD**, a brave African American, did not submit and surrender because of his color!

- **THOMAS JEFFERSON** did not stand for someone to think that they were above another when he helped write the Declaration of Independence!

- **BENJAMIN BANNEKER**, an African American, did not allow his fears to stop him from writing our leaders about ending slavery here in America.

- **MARTIN LUTHER KING, JR.** did not give in when he saw something that was not right!

Nor did

- **BILLY GRAHAM** has never wavered from his commitment to serve God.

Throughout history many men and women have persevered and overcome tough situations because they put their trust in God rather than allowing the world to hold them back. No matter who we are or where we have been it is vital to recognize that God is the one who picks us up and lays us down to serve His purpose and not our own! The Lord gives us our inner confidence and drive that will not sway in this world until our job is done. It is our place to do the best we can every day that we have been given. When we live our lives as an example under Christ it teaches our children, family, and friends to never lose hope—*no matter what they have to face.* Because with God "All Things Are Possible," even when the world seems to be falling apart!

In the persistence of men and women who never give up we can clearly see God at work and have faith that God will make a positive difference for our future! I challenge you today and every other day to strengthen yourself in the Lord and allow the love of Jesus to shine in your life like never before! It is when we know that *Greater Is He that Is In Us Than He That Is In This World* that we will find strength to overcome all of the obstacles in our lives! Never lose hope no matter what you face or what you have been through because when we let go of ourselves God will take over and carry us to new levels in His boundless mercy and grace." PUSH!!!

BIBLIOGRAPHY

A.W. Tozer. *The Purpose of Man: Designed to Worship.* California: Regal, 2009.

Cho Yonggi, David. Unleashing the Power of Faith. Korean: Bridge-Logos Publishers, 2006.

Evans, Tony. *Victory in Spiritual Warfare.* Eugene, Oregon: Harvest House Publishers, 2011.

Giglio, Louie. *The Air I Breathe.* Colorado Springs: Multnomah Books, 2006.

Hagin, Kenneth. *Learning to Flow With the Spirit of God.* Kindle book: Kenneth Hagin Ministries, 1986.

Hill, Cherie. *WAITING on GOD.* Kindle book: CreateSpace Independent Publishing Platform, 2012.

Hitz, Shelley. *21 Stories of Gratitude: The Power of Living Life With a Grateful Heart (A Life of Gratitude).* Kindle book: Body and Soul Publishing, 2012.

Harrison, James. *The Persistence Of God That Changes The World.* http://balancedlifeministry.org. February 13th, 2010.

Munroe, Myles. *The Purpose and Power of Praise & Worship.* Shippensburg: Destiny Image Publishers, 2000.

Meyer, Joyce. *Battlefield of the Mind.* New York: FaithWords; Revised edition, 2002.

Merritt, James. Sermon; HELP! http://www.sermonoutlines.org

Oyedepo, David. *Pillars Of Destiny.* Nigeria: Dominion Publishing House, 1st edition, 2008.

Osteen, Joel. *It's Your Time.* New York: Free Press; Reprint edition, 2010.

Oyedepo, David. *Understanding the power of praise.* Nigeria: Dominion Publishing House, 2005.

Omartian, Stormie, *Just Enough Light for the Step I'm On.* Eugene, Oregon: Harvest House Publishers, 2008.

Oral, Roberts. *When You See The Invisible, You Can Do The Impossible.* Shippensburg: Destiny Image Publishers, 2005.

Prince, Derek. *Promise of Provision.* Minnesota: Chosen Books, 2011.

Redman, Matt. The Unquenchable Worshipper. California: Regal, 2001.

T.D. Jakes. *Ten Commandments of Working in a Hostile Environment*. New York: Berkley Hardcover; First edition, 2005.

T.D. Jakes. *It Will All Come out in the Fire*. DVD. USA: Goldhill Home Media, 2007.

T.D. Jakes. *Why? Because You Are Anointed*. Shippensburg: Destiny Image Publishers, 2008.

Warren, Rick. *God's Power to Change Your Life*. Michigan: Zondervan; Supersaver edition, 2006.

ACKNOWLEDGMENTS

First, I would like to thank my Heavenly Father and Jesus Christ our Lord and Savior for originating and orchestrating this book. Also for giving me the strength, wisdom, knowledge, and understand to write it.

Thanks to my lovely wife Laetitia Bonsu. Titia, thanks for your understanding and supporting this work. For sparking the conversation that would lead to me writing this book. I can always count on you to support whatever project I have in mind. I appreciate it more than you know.

To my two princesses (Daughters); Janelle Kierra and Janessa Kimani BONSU, you girls ROCK! You are wonderful gift from God. Daddy loves you!!!

I'm so grateful to all the teachers and encouragers God has blessed us to walk with and learn from — Ps. Yvan Castanou (Your passion and vision inspire me), Bishop John and Penny Francis, Noel Robinson, Ps. Matthew Ashimolowo, Bishop David Oyedepo, Ps. Ransford Obeng, Bishop N. Jones, Ps. Mensa Otabil, Bishop Tudor Bismark (Thanks for your insight), Ps. Yves Castanou (You gave me the passion for reading, I dedicate this book to your leadership sir!) and all the ministers at ICC.

A massive thanks to Jerry Bonsu Ministries team, VLIC family, and Levitical Anointing group for believing in me and encouraging me at every moment. Your combined effort has brought me to this point and I'm sure and hope we still have so many more positive and fun journeys to experience together. Not only are we touching lives and building futures but making history.

Thanks to Carole, Kemi, Sabrina, Eric, Dianké, Luck, Eddy and Mateta for your response to the chapter I sent you. I value your opinion very much. Thanks to the

Nsilulu family. To "Willy" for the back cover picture. Big thanks to Lena (Christian Author Services), Scoot Philip Stewart for editing, proof reading the book and giving me honest feedback. I also would like to thank Lisa (www.lionsgatebookdesign.com) for designing the cover of this book.

And finally, thanks to all my friends and family for their love and supporting everything I want to do in my life. Thanks to my Pop! Mr. Bonsu what can I say old man…lol. Love you Pop! Hey Papa! My other Pop, thanks for believing in me! Special thanks to my Mom and my auntie Comfort for guiding my life and teaching me all that I know and training my mind to think outside of the box and teaching me how to articulate the feelings of my heart. I love you both so much and I appreciate everything you have done for me. I want to say a big thanks to my mother in law "Mame Lea", you're like a mother to me, thanks for your love and support. To my Granny; Nana, for your inspiring parts of this book and adding insight to my life. R. I. P. Nana… You are missed.

Peace and abundant blessings to all.

ABOUT THE AUTHOR

Determined, Innovative, Anointed, and Cutting Edge are some words often used to describe **JERRY BONSU**. He is the founder of Victory Life International Center (VLIC), a revolutionary Movement of 'like minded' and 'like spirited' people coming together in one accord: whose mission is to empower and equip individuals through teaching and preaching the uncompromised Word of God, and helping them to fulfill their highest calling and usher them into a supernatural lifestyle of faith and abundant living.

Jerry is also the visionary and founder behind several entities, including: Victory in Praise International Gathering, a vibrant, dynamic worship conference, which brings together more than 2000 people each gathering, — a wide audience of pastors, worship leaders, artists, musicians, scholars, students, and other interested worshipers. Founder and President of Jerry Bonsu Ministries (JBM); Leader of a gospel group Jerry Bonsu & Levitical Anointing; And the co-founder of a non-profit organization Elyon Foundation, created to influence the next generation.

Jerry — dynamic conference speaker, author, life coach, entrepreneur, worship leader… also travels throughout the world with his breakthrough teaching on understanding your God-given identity, purpose, and destiny in Christ. His mission is to impact his generation with divine revelation. Jerry and his wife, Laetitia are the proud parents of two children, Janelle Kierra and Janessa Kimani.

BOOKS & CD'S BY JERRY BONSU

* *The Power Of I AM (Book)*
* *The Power Of I AM (Audio Book)*
* *The Path to Victory (Book)*
* *Victory Noise (Music Album)*

Order these inspiring products and more by visiting www.jerrybonsu.org and be sure to join this movement on Facebook & Twitter.

WWW.JERRYBONSU.ORG

www.ingramcontent.com/pod-product-compliance
Lightning Source LLC
Chambersburg PA
CBHW071508040426
42444CB00008B/1553